"Coming together is a beginning. Keeping together is progress. Working together is success."

—HENRY FORD

SECRETS *From* GRANDMA'S ATTIC

SECRETS *from* GRANDMA'S ATTIC

Veiled Intentions

Gabrielle Meyer

Published by Guideposts
100 Reserve Road, Suite E200
Danbury, CT 06810
Guideposts.org

Cover and interior design by Müllerhaus
Cover illustration by Greg Copeland represented at Online Illustration LLC.
Typeset by Aptara, Inc.

ISBN 978-1-961125-91-9 (hardcover)
ISBN 978-1-961125-92-6 (epub)

Printed and bound in the United States of America
10 9 8 7 6 5 4 3 2 1

Veiled Intentions

Chapter One

$\mathcal{A}$ gentle snow fell from the dark clouds outside Amy Allen's house. The temperature had fallen throughout the day, but Amy hardly noticed as she sat at the cozy dinner table with her combined family. Her fiancé, Miles Anderson, met her gaze from across the table, and they shared a quiet smile. Their children competed to tell them about the snowball fight that had left them all rosy-faced and happy.

"The girls won," seven-year-old Jana said, making a face at the boys. Jana was Amy's adopted daughter, and she was the same age as Miles's daughter, Natalie. The two girls were best friends and already called themselves sisters, although the wedding was still three weeks away.

"No way," Matt said. He looked to Colton for confirmation. "We threw more snowballs and hit you more than you hit us."

Matt was Jana's brother, and he and Colton were both eleven and in the same class at Canton Elementary School. Though their relationship had gotten off to a rocky start, they were good friends now. Maybe not as excited to become brothers as the girls were to become sisters, but they still looked forward to the new family adventure.

"I don't think it really matters who won," Miles said. "I'm just happy you were outside enjoying yourselves. What else did you do in the snow?"

Natalie began to tell him all about the snow angels she and Jana had made while the boys talked about building snowmen.

Amy watched and listened, marveling that in three short weeks she, Matt, and Jana would move in with Miles and his kids and they'd start their lives together. Finally. After dating in high school and then breaking up before going to college, Amy and Miles had gone their separate ways for over thirty years. But both had returned to their hometown of Canton, Missouri, about the same time. Amy as a single mom to two adopted children and Miles as a single, divorced dad. Their friendship had quickly rekindled, though their romance had taken a little more time to develop. But Amy wouldn't change a thing. It had all happened exactly how God had orchestrated, and they would soon be married.

"Who's ready for dessert?" Amy asked when she heard the oven timer ding. The noise made Scrappy bark. Miles and Amy had recently purchased the little black, white, and brown ball of fur with floppy ears. He had been enjoying shared company with both families but would soon live full-time with the whole family at Miles's house.

A unanimous chorus rose to accompany Scrappy's barks.

"I'll help," Miles said. He stood and joined Amy in the kitchen.

The kids continued to talk in animated voices about the snow, hoping more would fall over the weekend so that school would be canceled on Monday morning.

"Supper was great," Miles said as he went to the freezer and took out the vanilla ice cream he had brought to Amy's house for their dessert.

Amy opened the oven and pulled out the pan of brownies, shooing Scrappy away. The chocolate aroma filled the kitchen and made her stomach rumble, despite just having eaten supper.

"Thanks." Amy knew Miles loved lasagna, so she had made it just for him.

"I see you've started to pack." Miles motioned to a stack of boxes near the back door.

"Those are things I'm donating to the thrift store, but I have started to pack." She couldn't hide her excitement as she set the brownies on the counter.

Miles approached her and slipped his arms around her, pulling her close.

Amy hugged him back. They would be living in the same house together in three short weeks. Miles's home was a large Victorian, not far from her sister Tracy. It was easily twice as big as Amy's house and filled with so many good memories already. She would miss this house, but she was eager to make a new home.

"I'm literally crossing the days off on my calendar," Miles said with a grin.

Amy smiled and left his arms to take a knife out of the drawer to cut the brownies. "I signed papers with the Realtor yesterday. She said that things are a little slow right now, but she's hopeful that by spring we'll have the house sold. I let her know we're not in any hurry. As long as we get the necessities moved into your house by the wedding, we can take our time moving the rest out afterward. I won't mind if it takes a little bit of time to sell my house."

Amy cut into the brownies though they were still piping hot. She lifted the gooey dessert into serving bowls, and Miles dropped a scoop of ice cream into each. They carried them into the dining room and were met with cheers.

Everyone made quick work of the dessert, and then the kids cleared their plates. They took Scrappy into the living room, where they attempted to teach him how to sit, roll over, and fetch, leaving Miles and Amy at the table to talk.

They were discussing wedding plans when Amy's phone rang.

Amy stood and returned to the kitchen where her cell phone was charging on the counter. When she picked it up, she saw her Realtor's number.

"Hello?" she said.

"Hi, Amy, this is Carol Molenkamp."

"Hi, Carol. How are you?"

"I'm great—perfect, actually. I have some wonderful news for you."

"Oh?"

"You got an offer on your house today!"

Amy frowned, confused. "What do you mean? You haven't even shown it yet."

"The buyer contacted me this morning, looking for a house that fit the description of yours perfectly. She lives in Florida and doesn't have the opportunity to come and see it in person, so I sent her the pictures I took yesterday. She loved it and made a cash offer."

It took Amy a moment to process everything Carol had just said. She left the kitchen and joined Miles in the dining room. He looked at her curiously.

"There's been an offer on the house," Amy said to him.

He grinned and gave her a thumbs-up.

"The buyer is offering above asking price too," Carol continued.

"What?" Amy could hardly believe it.

"But there's a catch." Carol's voice grew serious.

"Okay." Amy took the seat across from Miles and said, "Carol, can I put you on speaker so Miles can listen in?"

"Of course."

Amy lowered her phone and placed it on speaker. "Go ahead, Carol."

"Sure. I was just telling Amy that she's had a cash offer on her house from a buyer in Florida. The buyer has offered above asking price, but there's a caveat." She paused and took a deep breath. "She'll need you to close on the house in two weeks."

Amy's jaw dropped. "Two weeks? That's impossible. We're getting married in three weeks, and I'm in the middle of planning the wedding. I couldn't possibly move out of my house in two weeks. Couldn't we make it at least a month?"

"The buyer needs the house in two weeks. She's moving from Florida and needs somewhere to live when she gets here. It's a non-negotiable closing date."

Amy looked at Miles.

He simply shrugged.

"Carol, can Miles and I discuss this and call you back?"

"Of course. I'll email you the details, and you can take some time to talk things through. I'll need an answer by tomorrow morning though, because if you aren't willing to accept the offer, then the buyer will need to keep looking. She has a job starting here in two weeks."

"I understand. Thanks. I'll let you know first thing in the morning."

"Okay. Bye, you two. I look forward to hearing from you."

"Bye," Amy and Miles both said before Amy ended the call.

Amy studied Miles as he smiled at her.

"Wow," he said, "that was unexpected."

Amy took a deep breath. "I don't even know what to say. I didn't think this would happen so quickly."

"The offer is great," Miles said. "And the extra money would be nice."

"I have been wanting to start a college fund for Matt and Jana." Amy paused. "For all the kids."

Miles reached across the table and took her hand. "It takes some getting used to, doesn't it? The idea of sharing everything. Finances, kids, plans—"

"Dreams," she finished with a smile, and then grew serious again. "Do you think we could move out of here in two weeks? There's so much to do with the wedding and moving into your house—I'm not sure it's possible."

"I'm free every evening," he said. "And we can ask your family for help. I know Tracy and Robin will be here every opportunity they can get."

Amy's sister, Tracy, and their cousin, Robin, were her two best friends. If she asked them, she knew they'd help.

"It sounds like you think this is a good idea," she said.

He let go of her hand and nodded. "I know it'll be tough, but I think we can do it. I don't want to miss an opportunity for you to sell the house for top dollar. I think it'll be worth the extra work in the end."

Amy nibbled her bottom lip. If she was doing it by herself, she'd have to say no. But with Miles's help, and the possibility of her sister's and cousin's help too, she felt more confident.

"Okay. I'll let Carol know in the morning that we'll accept the offer. And I'll see if the kids and I can stay with Tracy and Jeff for the week between the sale and the wedding. She has lots of space, and I know she won't mind."

Miles grinned and stood.

He reached out to Amy, and she stood. "Congratulations," he said as he pulled her close. "We're about to be a one-home family."

Amy laid her cheek against Miles's chest, excited and a little apprehensive. It was all happening so quickly. She just hoped she didn't regret saying yes to the offer.

Amy felt distracted the next morning as she entered the church with Matt and Jana for Sunday school. The kids ran off to their classrooms, and Amy hung her jacket on the coatrack.

"Hey," Tracy said as she came up behind Amy. "What's this about you selling your house?"

Amy turned to her older sister just as their cousin, Robin, walked up to join them.

"You sold your house?" Robin asked with big eyes.

"How did you hear?" Amy asked Tracy.

"Jana just told me as she ran by me on her way to class."

Amy smiled and shook her head. "She's like the town crier."

"Is it true?" Robin asked.

"It's true. I called Carol Molenkamp this morning before we came to church." Amy quickly filled them in on the particulars.

"How are you feeling?" Tracy asked.

"A little worried and apprehensive," Amy admitted. "But also excited and ready to be done and move on to the next phase of my life."

Miles entered the church with Colton and Natalie. The kids ran off to their classrooms while Miles joined Amy, Tracy, and Robin.

"Amy just told us the good news," Tracy said to Miles after everyone greeted each other. "I say we should all head over to Amy's right after Sunday lunch to get started on packing."

"You guys don't need to come over on your day off," Amy protested.

"I'll pretty much be at your house every waking minute these next two weeks," Tracy warned. "And Jeff will help when he can. We have a lot of work to do."

Amy didn't realize just how much she was hoping her sister would help. Relief flooded her, and she gave Tracy a big hug. "Thank you."

"Of course."

The morning went by quickly, and soon Amy, Miles, and the kids pulled up to Tracy's house for their weekly Sunday meal.

Tracy and her husband, Jeff, had inherited Grandma Pearl's beautiful Victorian home when Grandma passed away two years ago. In the recently fallen snow, it was especially beautiful. A large turret, bay windows, and a wraparound porch were some of the features that made it remarkable, but it was the years of family memories within that made it special. Tracy and Jeff were the third generation to own the home, and it was full of priceless treasures and mysteries from decades of family life.

The kids greeted each other after they pulled up in two different vehicles as if they hadn't just spent the morning together at church. They ran into the house even before Amy and Miles had met on the sidewalk out front.

Miles reached for Amy's hand, and they walked to the house together.

Tracy greeted them at the door with a big smile. "Come on in. Lunch will be ready soon."

Robin was already there with her husband, Terry, and their fifteen-year-old son, Kai. Miles and Amy took off their outer gear, and Matt, Colton, and Kai left to find a board game to play.

"It smells delicious in here," Amy said.

"Jeff made his famous meat loaf," Tracy said. "I'm making mashed potatoes and gravy."

"I brought a salad," Robin added.

"And I have dessert," Amy said. She held up the pan of chocolate cake she had made the previous night and frosted that morning.

"Great." Tracy stood back and waited until everyone had their coats hung up. "Miles and Terry, I'm wondering if you'd be willing to help Jeff out in the kitchen while I take Amy and Robin on a little treasure hunt in the attic."

"Oh?" Amy handed Miles the chocolate cake. "What kind of treasure hunt?"

Tracy shrugged. "It's a secret."

Amy frowned, curious about what her sister was up to.

Miles winked at her as he left the entryway and moved toward the kitchen with Terry at his side.

Robin and Amy followed Tracy up the stairs to the second floor. "What is this about?" Robin asked. "I had a feeling you didn't want to say anything in front of the guys."

Tracy smiled as she walked toward the guest room. The stairs to the attic were inside the bedroom closet.

"There are only three weeks until Amy's wedding," Tracy said with her hand on the doorknob. "And now that we're going to be busy packing up her house, I thought we better find the family veil to get it aired out for the wedding."

Amy paused before she entered the room, her heart warming. "I almost forgot! How could I forget?"

Tracy and Robin smiled at Amy—their excitement for her wedding almost as keen as hers.

The family wedding veil had first been worn by Great-grandma Vivian at her wedding. It was a gorgeous veil with a delicate, pearl-lined headpiece and long, cathedral-length netting. After Great-grandma Vivian wore it, Grandma Pearl had worn it, and her daughter, Ruth—Robin's mother—had been the third bride. Both Robin and Tracy had worn it, and the last to wear it was Tracy's daughter, Sara.

"You'll be the seventh bride to wear the veil," Tracy said, smiling at Amy. "Six very happy marriages have preceded you—and I know the seventh will be just as joyful and blessed."

Tears sprang to Amy's eyes.

The bedroom light was turned on, and the closet door was already open. The sound of Jana and Natalie's giggles could be heard coming from the attic.

"It sounds like the girls have beat us to it," Tracy said.

"Remember when we used to play up there?" Amy asked.

"Some of my happiest memories took place up there," Robin said. "Playing dress-up in Grandma Pearl's old bridesmaid dresses."

The three of them walked up the steep steps to the attic. A bare lightbulb hung overhead, and piles of furniture, covered with dust-covers, were scattered throughout the room. There were boxes, rubber storage bins, old trunks filled with treasures, and several generations of family heirlooms.

"What are you two doing up here?" Amy asked when she got to the top of the stairs.

"We're playing with Grandma Pearl's dollhouse," Natalie said with a grin.

Robin and Tracy smiled at Amy, and she could almost tell what they were thinking. They loved that Natalie already thought of Grandma Pearl as her own, even though Miles and Amy weren't married yet.

"What are you doing up here?" Jana asked as she moved one of the dolls from the parlor to the dining room.

"We're up here looking for a very special wedding veil," Tracy said. She moved to a bookcase where several family photo albums were stored. "I'll show you some pictures of it."

The girls went to Tracy's side and waited for her to find the right album. When she did, she took a seat on one of the cloth-covered chairs and opened it for them.

"This is your great-great-grandmother Vivian," Tracy said, pointing to the picture of Vivian in her wedding dress and veil.

"Oh, she's pretty," Natalie said. "But she looks kind of weird."

"This picture was taken over a hundred years ago. They dressed differently than us, didn't they?" Tracy asked.

The girls nodded.

"This is the veil she wore on her wedding day," Tracy said. "And then..." She flipped a few pages and showed them Grandma Pearl. "Your great-grandma Pearl wore it when she got married in 1945. And then"—she turned another page—"Aunt Ruth wore it, and I wore it, and Robin wore it, and Sara wore it."

The girls' eyes were wide as they studied the pictures.

Natalie looked up at Tracy. "Can I wear it some day?"

"And me?" Jana asked.

Tracy grinned at the girls and nodded. "Of course!"

Amy's heart warmed at the scene.

"Where is it?" Natalie asked.

"It's in the trunk over there." Tracy rose and led the girls to the wedding trunk in the corner of the attic. "We're taking it out so Amy can wear it on her wedding day."

The little girls looked up at Amy with wide eyes.

Inside the wedding trunk they'd stored Great-grandma Vivian's and Grandma Pearl's wedding gowns along with the veil and a few other odds and ends. Amy hadn't seen the veil since Sara's wedding, six years ago, but she remembered it well.

"Sara's wedding was the last one that Grandma Pearl attended," Amy suddenly realized. "I wish she could be here for mine."

"At least you have her veil," Jana said.

Amy chuckled at the simple response. "You're right. Grandma Pearl is here with us through our memories."

Tracy moved some framed pictures off the top of the trunk and opened the lid. It squeaked on its hinges and revealed several boxes within.

Slowly, she removed each box and set them aside, but then she paused.

"I don't see the veil box."

"What?" Amy frowned, getting closer. "What do you mean?"

"It's not in here."

"Maybe it got put in one of the other boxes inside the trunk," Robin suggested.

Tracy, Amy, and Robin opened each box, revealing gowns, gloves, shoes, and other items, but there was no veil.

"How is this possible?" Tracy asked. "I know I returned the veil to this trunk after Sara wore it. I remember specifically. I had it professionally cleaned and stored in an archival box, and then I brought it up here and put it in this trunk."

Robin shrugged. "Maybe it got moved."

"Where?" Tracy asked. "And who would have moved it?"

"I don't know," Robin said. "Maybe Grandma Pearl?"

Disappointment weighed heavily on Amy's heart. All her life, she'd been looking forward to the day she might wear the wedding veil. What if they couldn't find it?

"Did someone steal it?" Jana asked, frowning and clearly upset.

"Surely not." Tracy shook her head. "Who would want to steal the family wedding veil? It can't have any monetary value. It's more of a priceless family heirloom."

"Something happened to it," Amy said. "It couldn't have just disappeared into thin air. Someone must know where it went."

Robin nodded. "We'll find it, Amy. You're right, it has to be somewhere."

Amy couldn't help but wonder what she would wear if they couldn't find the veil in time.

But, more importantly, where had it gone?

Chapter Two

All Amy could think about on Monday during work was getting home to start packing. As a first-grade teacher at Canton Elementary School, however, she needed to stay focused to get through the day. Her young students were especially rambunctious and hard to keep on task.

But as soon as the last bell rang, Amy was ready to head home and focus her attention on her house.

Miles was a family doctor and worked at the Blessings Convenient Care Clinic until three each day so he could be available for his children after school. He and Amy had already planned on her taking all four kids home and meeting him at her house. They would spend the evening packing and order pizza for supper.

Canton Elementary wasn't a large school, so it didn't take long for Jana and Natalie to meander into Amy's classroom, chattering about something that had happened on the playground.

Amy greeted them and continued to pack her bag with some papers she needed to take home that evening.

Soon, Matt was in her classroom—but no Colton.

"Where is Colton?" Amy asked as she put her empty coffee mug into her bag.

Matt shrugged and set his backpack on a desk.

"Wasn't he in class with you?"

"Yeah."

"Then where did he go? We need to get home as soon as we can. Miles is meeting us there."

"I don't know where he went."

"Is he in the restroom?"

"I don't think so."

Amy was already feeling a little frazzled from the hectic day and the looming work ahead of her. She didn't feel like interrogating Matt. "When was the last time you saw him?"

"When I was getting my coat and backpack. He was taking things out of his desk."

Amy sighed and put her coat on. No doubt Colton would be there any second.

After she put on her scarf and mittens, she grabbed her backpack and her lunch bag. "Let's wait for him in the hallway."

She turned off the lights and left her room with the kids in tow.

The hallway was almost empty, with no sign of Colton.

"Where is he?" she asked again. "Let's walk to your classroom and see if he got held up there, Matt. Maybe your teacher needed to talk to him."

Matt, Jana, and Natalie followed Amy down the hall to the boys' classroom. The teacher was still there, grading papers. She looked up and smiled at Amy.

"Hey," Amy said. "Is Colton here?"

"No. He left with the other students a few minutes ago."

Amy frowned. "That's strange. He knew he was supposed to meet me in my room."

"He's probably in the restroom," she suggested.

Amy and the kids trooped to the restroom next. Matt went in to check and came out shaking his head. "He's not in there either."

Apprehension wrapped around Amy's heart as her imagination started to run with possibilities. Where could he have gone?

They went back to her room, but he wasn't there. They went into the lunchroom and she glanced out at the empty playground, and still, no Colton.

She was about to call Miles when they finally found him standing outside the front doors.

Amy's legs felt weak with relief. "Colton!"

He looked up at her with a blank expression.

"What are you doing out here? I told you to meet me in my classroom after the last bell."

He shrugged, much like Matt had done.

"Why didn't you come with Matt?"

"I don't know." Colton pushed away from the wall. "Sorry," he said, though he didn't appear remorseful.

Amy took a deep breath and put her arm around him for a quick hug. "I'm just happy you're okay. But next time you need to meet me where I tell you. Okay?"

He nodded and pulled away from her.

A new kind of apprehension tightened her heart. Just last month, they'd dealt with Jana's misgivings about the upcoming wedding and the two families becoming one. Were they going to have to do the same with Colton? With her house selling, it was getting very real—for all of them.

"Come on," Amy said, choosing not to dwell on the situation. "We have a lot of work to do, and we need to meet your dad at my house."

They piled into Amy's car, with Colton, as the oldest and biggest, in the front seat with her.

Amy wished that all four kids could ride in the back where it was safer. Was it time for her to get a bigger car? Like a minivan?

The thought surprised Amy and reminded her that she was again about to make a very big change in her life. There had been an adjustment from being a single woman to a mom with two kids. And now she was about to be married with four kids. There were bound to be some growing pains.

She drove the short distance to her house. Miles waited in his Jeep, which was parked on the street, so Amy pulled into her detached garage, and everyone piled out.

The kids ran to the house to let Scrappy out as Amy met Miles in the snowy yard. He gave her a kiss and smiled at her.

"Hi."

"Hi," she said. Though she was happy to see him, she was still a little upset about Colton's disappearance. She told Miles what had happened.

"I don't think it's a big deal," she said, "but you might want to talk to him."

Miles put his arm around Amy's shoulders and walked with her toward the house. "I will. Thanks for telling me."

They entered the kitchen, and Amy set down her backpack. Her eye caught on a note she had written to herself the day before and left on her refrigerator. "Ugh. I forgot to call the woman making our cake. I need to see if she can bake gluten-free cupcakes for

Anna. It's probably a good idea to have enough in case other people need them too."

Anna was married to Chad, Tracy's son. She had recently discovered she was gluten intolerant.

"Go ahead and call her now," Miles said. "I'll get a snack for the kids and then have them help me unload the boxes I picked up at the grocery store. How does that sound?"

"Perfect. I'll help you as soon as I'm finished."

Amy took her cell phone into her home office where she did most of her work. She kept her wedding folder on the desk. It was a three-ring binder with the names and phone numbers of all her wedding vendors. She had been keeping track of everything in there—receipts, notes, and ideas. It was color-coded, with tabs for each vendor, and a detailed to-do list for each week, and then each day, leading up to the big event.

But the binder wasn't on the desk.

Frowning, Amy looked in the drawers and then went into the living room to check in there. Had she left it somewhere else? She thought back and tried to remember when she had used it last. It had been several days.

The kids were just coming in with Scrappy, so she walked into the kitchen and said, "Matt? Jana? Have you seen my wedding folder?"

Matt and Jana shook their heads.

"Anyone else?" she asked Miles, Colton, and Natalie.

Everyone shook their heads.

"The last time I saw it was when you brought it to my house a couple weeks ago," Miles said.

"Hmm." Amy frowned again. "I'll check my bedroom."

She went to her room but couldn't find it there either.

Tracy and Robin planned to be at her house by three thirty, so she couldn't spend too long looking for it. No doubt it would show up as they started to pack.

Amy searched for the bakery's number online, and she was soon dialing the number.

"Hello, Cake Creations. This is Trish. How can I help you?"

"Hi, Trish," Amy said. "This is Amy Allen. I have a wedding cake ordered for the end of this month. I'm wondering if I can add an order of gluten-free cupcakes."

"Oh." Trish sounded surprised for some reason. "Let me pull up your information and check a couple of things."

Amy waited in silence until Trish spoke again.

"Hmm. I found your order, but I have a note here that you canceled it."

"What?" Amy sat on her bed and looked out the window. "That can't be right. I placed my order weeks ago. I didn't cancel it."

"I remember when you placed your order," Trish said, "but I also remember when you canceled it."

"That's impossible."

"I made a note. You called on the third. I remember the conversation."

"There must be a mistake." Amy stood and paced to the window. "I didn't cancel the order. I didn't call you last week."

"I'm so sorry about this," Trish said, sounding truly apologetic. "Someone called and canceled your order."

"It's okay." Amy tried to stay calm. Sometimes mistakes happened. "I guess it's a good thing I called then. I'll need to place my order again."

There was another pause. "Unfortunately, someone else called just a few days ago and placed a substantial order for the same weekend. Since I run this business on my own, I won't have enough time to meet both of your needs. I'm very, very sorry."

Amy was speechless for a moment, surprised to hear this. She'd been very careful in selecting a baker and had loved the samples she'd tried from Trish.

"I'm—I'm confused," she finally said. "I don't know how this happened."

"Again, I'm sorry."

"And there's no way you can fit my order in?"

"No. The other order that came in is a significant one. I'll be lucky if I can get it done by myself."

"Okay." Amy's disappointment cut deep. "What about my deposit?"

There was another awkward pause. "If you remember, it was nonrefundable."

"But I didn't cancel the order."

"I'm so sorry. I don't know what to say."

Amy didn't want to be difficult. Thankfully, the deposit wasn't large. It didn't pay to make a stink. She had three weeks before the wedding. Surely she could find someone else by then. "Thank you for your time."

She hung up just as Miles poked his head into her bedroom. "Everything okay?"

"No. Someone canceled our wedding cake order, and Trish can't honor our request anymore." She quickly explained the conversation they'd had. "I'll have to find someone else."

Miles entered her room and drew her into a hug. "There's still time."

"I know, but I was really looking forward to Trish's work. Her cakes are gorgeous."

"We'll find someone just as talented."

Amy nodded, though she highly doubted it.

"But," Miles said, "maybe you should call your other vendors to confirm plans."

"That's a good idea. If I can find my binder, I have everyone's numbers listed."

"I'll help you look."

Amy smiled at him. "Thank you."

"You're welcome."

Amy was disappointed—but at least she was still marrying Miles. At the end of the day, that was the most important thing to keep in mind.

She just hoped she could find a new baker in time.

"I don't understand," Amy said twenty minutes later as Tracy and Robin stood in her living room. The kids were upstairs going through their toys with Natalie's and Colton's help. "Someone called my vendors and told them they were me and canceled my entire wedding! And many of my deposits were nonrefundable, so I'm also out all that money."

"What?" Tracy said. "Why would someone do that?"

"I don't know. But I suspect that whoever did it was also the person who called back a couple days later and booked each of them for their own wedding—on the same day as ours."

"They're all booked?" Robin asked.

"Yes—the reception hall, the caterer, the photographer, the baker, and the florist!" Amy hadn't felt this frustrated or angry in a long time. "I don't know what I'm going to do. It took weeks to secure all of them, and with only three weeks left till the wedding, I don't know if I'll be able to find replacements."

Miles stood next to Amy, listening as she ranted to her sister and cousin. He was just as frustrated as she was.

"Did you ask your vendors who the person was?" Tracy asked.

"I tried, but no one was willing to tell me the names of their customers—which I get—but, sheesh! I'm assuming this was done by the same person. They probably got engaged after me and I had all their vendors selected and they decided to be underhanded. I'd like to find whoever this is and give them a piece of my mind." Amy crossed her arms, trying not to cry. How was she supposed to fix this? And who would do something like this to her?

"There has to be a way to figure out who it is," Robin said.

Miles put his arms around Amy and held her as she tried to pull herself together. This couldn't have happened at a worse time. She needed to focus her energy on moving. The purchase agreement had already been signed, and there was no way to back out now.

"Do you want to postpone the wedding?" Miles asked softly.

Amy looked up at him, tears stinging her eyes. "No. Do you?"

"No." He shook his head. "I'd marry you in jeans and a T-shirt, in my living room, with a homemade cake and picture on a cell phone, if it came to that. I want you to have the wedding of your dreams, Amy, but at the end of the day, all I really want is for you to be my wife."

Amy smiled through her tears. "You're right. That's all that matters."

"We can still plan a beautiful wedding," Tracy said. "It might take some work and some creativity, but we can do it."

"You're already helping so much," Amy protested as she pulled out of Miles's embrace and wiped her cheeks. "I couldn't ask you to do more."

"Oh, hush," Tracy said, hugging Amy. "What's family for, if not to help in emergencies? We've got this, Amy."

Robin hugged Amy next. "We'll do whatever it takes. I promise."

Amy smiled at her sister and cousin. "Okay. Let's focus on packing tonight, and tomorrow I'll start looking for new wedding vendors. And if you happen to find my wedding binder, please let me know. I can't find it anywhere."

"You can't find your wedding binder?" Tracy asked with a frown. "The book you've been carrying around for weeks? Do you think that whoever canceled your vendors got ahold of it somehow?"

"I don't know." Amy frowned. "I hadn't even thought of that."

"Who would want to sabotage our wedding?" Miles asked. "It doesn't make any sense."

"Do you think this is personal?" Amy asked him. "You don't think some random person just wanted the same day we had?"

"It feels personal, doesn't it?"

Amy's head started to hurt, and they hadn't even begun to pack yet.

"Don't worry about all that right now," Robin said. "Let's concentrate on one thing at a time. Where would you like us to start?"

Amy closed her eyes for a second to try to refocus on the task at hand. "How about we start with decorations, pictures, knick-knacks, things like that?"

"Perfect." Robin nodded. "I'll tackle the living room."

"And we need to figure out what furniture you want to move to Miles's house," Tracy said. "Do you know what you want to do with the rest of it?"

Miles's house was fully furnished, but he had told Amy that she should bring anything she wanted or needed with her. They'd make room.

"I have a list," Amy said, more frustrated than before. "It's in my wedding binder. I've been keeping everything in there."

"That's okay," Miles said. "We'll just go through each room and start a new list."

Amy nodded. There was no point in bemoaning what they couldn't change right now.

An hour later, as she was putting framed pictures into a box, Amy remembered the wedding veil. "Any luck finding the veil?"

Tracy shook her head. "I wasn't going to say anything, since you're already overwhelmed. I looked everywhere I could think of and called all the family members who might have seen it, but I can't find it."

"It doesn't make any sense." Amy let out a sigh. It was really the least of her worries right now, but it was still disappointing and only added to her frustration.

"Maybe Grandma Pearl loaned it to someone," Robin suggested. "Just like we loaned the picture of Great-uncle Raymond to the historical society for the special exhibit on the Korean War that one time."

"I doubt she would have let someone else wear it," Tracy said.

"I do too," Robin agreed. "I'm just thinking about an exhibit or something."

"I suppose that's a possibility," Tracy said, though she sounded skeptical. "I can check with Tawny and see if she knows anything about it."

"That's a great plan." Amy nodded. She needed to believe that they had something solid to stand on—a possibility or a lead. Anything was better than giving up.

They continued to work for the next couple of hours, and Amy went from one room to the next, telling them which things she planned to take to Miles's house, which things could be sold, and which things would go in the donation pile.

It wasn't easy to decide what furniture to keep, since Miles really didn't need anything. But there were a few things, like Amy's piano, that meant a lot to her. A couple of her antiques would also go nicely in his Victorian home, but most of them could be sold or donated.

Scrappy was constantly underfoot, but the kids did their best to keep him out of the way. Amy suggested he should make the permanent move to Miles's house that evening.

When it was finally time to break for pizza, everyone was ready.

The smell of marinara sauce and garlic bread wafted through the air as they sat down at the dining room table.

"Thank you, everyone, for all your hard work," Amy said, taking a piece of pepperoni pizza. "I don't know what we'd do without you."

"I've had some time to think about your vendor predicament," Tracy said. "There aren't a lot of places to hold a wedding reception in Canton, so I'm trying to think outside the box."

"Yeah?" Amy leaned forward to grab a soda. "Do you have an idea?"

"What about the Museum of Wonders? They have an amazing space that could be used for a wedding."

"Do you think they'd let us rent it?" Amy asked.

"It's worth calling and asking."

The museum was housed in a beautiful historic building. Amy looked at Miles and raised her eyebrows.

"I've never been in there," Miles said. "I'd like to check it out."

"I'll call first and see if they're open to the idea," Amy said. "And if they are, we can schedule a visit."

"Sounds good to me. I'm pretty much willing to use any space we can find."

Amy smiled, feeling hopeful for the first time since talking to Trish.

"And I know a photographer," Robin said. "She specializes in still-life photography and likes to photograph antiques. I've used her for the shop before." Robin owned Pearls of Wisdom, an antique store in downtown Canton. "I could see if she's interested in doing a wedding."

"That would be great, Robin," Amy said. "Thank you."

"Of course."

They would have to be creative, but Amy was hopeful that they could still pull off a beautiful and memorable wedding. It might not be what she had pictured, but maybe it would be close.

Chapter Three

*F*or now," Miles said as they entered his house an hour later with boxes in hand, "let's store everything up in the attic. When we have more time to sort and organize, we can go through the boxes one at a time."

"That's a great idea." The box in Amy's arms was filled with the pictures she and Tracy had packed earlier. Behind her, entering the house, the kids carried boxes from Matt's and Jana's bedrooms. Scrappy was snug in Natalie's arms.

"Everyone up to the attic," Miles said. "Except Scrappy."

"I don't want my toys in the attic," Jana protested. "I want to put them in Natalie's room."

"I don't want Matt's things in my room," Colton said.

"But you and Matt are sharing a room," Miles said as he flipped on the light in the entryway.

The Victorian home was beautiful and had been lovingly cared for over the years. Miles had grown up in the house, but after he graduated from high school, his parents sold it and moved to St. Louis. When Miles came back to Canton a couple of years ago, he contacted the new owners and made an offer to buy it from them. They had been eager to sell, and now Miles owned his childhood home.

"I'm not sharing a room with Matt," Colton said, shaking his head. "No way!"

"I thought that's what we'd all decided," Amy said to him. "The girls would share a room, and the boys would share a room."

"I don't want to anymore." Colton kicked off his shoes. "Not with Matt or anyone else."

The house was large. A massive turret extended from the ground floor to the attic, which was more like a third floor, though it was mostly unfinished. There were two bedrooms up there that had once been used by maids but had gone into disrepair over the years and had been used as storage for decades. Bay windows, hidden alcoves, and gorgeous woodwork graced the house throughout the first and second floors.

The second floor had four bedrooms and two bathrooms. One of the rooms was Miles's home office and another was a guest room. Since the kids had wanted to share bedrooms, there hadn't been much talk about rearranging things. But now that Colton didn't want Matt in his room, they would need to discuss their options.

Jana linked arms with Natalie, who still held Scrappy, and the two little girls looked up at Amy and Miles. "We're sharing a room," Natalie said.

"I know," Amy said. "Your room is plenty big enough for the two of you."

"Where am I going to sleep?" Matt asked, looking a little worried.

"Not in my room," Colton said. He set down his box and marched up the stairs.

"I don't get a room?" Matt's gaze shifted from Amy to Miles.

"Of course you get a room, Matt," Miles told him. "This is going to be your house too."

Matt sat on the bottom step and put his elbows on his knees and his chin in his hands. "I don't want to move. If Colton doesn't want me here, I don't want to be here."

"Colton wants you here," Amy said, taking a seat next to Matt. "He's just having a little trouble right now with the adjustments."

"He's not the one moving again," Matt protested.

"Let's go put my dolls in your room," Jana said to Natalie as she started up the stairs.

"It's not just Natalie's room anymore," Miles reminded Jana. "You can say 'our room' from now on."

A funny look came over Natalie's face. "But it is my room, Daddy."

"Yes, but it's also Jana's room."

Natalie frowned. "It's my room, but Jana will sleep there."

"No, honey." Miles set his box down and crouched in front of his daughter. "It will be both of yours."

Scrappy wiggled, and Natalie put him down. Her bottom lip came out, and her frown deepened. "Mine."

Jana's mouth began to quiver, and tears sprang to her eyes. "I don't get a room?"

"You can stay with me," Matt said. "If I get a room."

Jana joined Matt on the step and cuddled close to him in an uncharacteristic moment of affection.

Amy's heart broke for them. They'd been through so much in their short lives. First with their troubled birth mother, then in foster care, and then adjusting to life in Canton with a new mom. Was this too much for them? She had thought they were excited to join the Anderson family, but now she wasn't so sure.

"Hey." Amy put her hand on Matt's back. "There's no reason to be sad. This is going to be our new forever home."

"That's what you said about the last house," Matt said.

Amy moved so that she was in front of her children. She put her hands on their knees and looked them in the eyes. "It's going to be okay, guys. I promise. It might take some adjustments for all of us, but this is going to be a wonderful home, where we're all going to make good memories together for the rest of our lives."

Miles took Natalie by the hand and led her over to Amy and the kids. He crouched down and motioned for Natalie to sit on the step next to Jana.

"I know this is hard," he said. "But we're a family now, and families make sacrifices for each other." He glanced up, and Amy's eyes followed his gaze.

Colton was sitting at the top of the steps.

Miles motioned for him to come down and join them.

Slowly, Colton came down and sat, a little distanced from the others.

Miles took Amy's hand and brought her to her feet.

"This isn't always going to be easy," he said. "But we promise we're going to work as hard as we can to make this home the best place it can possibly be for all of us. From this day forward, this house is now ours. It's not mine, it's not yours. It belongs to all of us. We will respect each other's boundaries, and there's enough space for everyone to have their own room, if they'd like. But I don't want anyone to say this is 'my' house. I want to hear you all say 'our' house from now on. Understand?"

Four heads nodded in unison.

"Good. Now, let's figure out the room situation." Miles looked at Amy. "What do you think?"

She still felt a little strange making decisions about Miles's house, but he was right. She needed to start thinking about it as their house.

"We can always fix up the bedrooms in the attic and use those for a guest room and a home office. That way, the bedrooms on the second floor could be used for the kids."

Miles smiled. "I've been thinking about the attic space too. Maybe we should think about finishing up the main room as a kids' rec room."

"Can I sleep in the attic?" Colton asked, his eyes wide.

"Me too?" Matt asked. "That sounds cool."

The boys were getting a little older, and they would be wanting more privacy.

Miles shrugged. "It wouldn't take much work to get those bedrooms ready. I could call around and see if someone would be willing to give me a bid. We can have them bid the rec room too."

"And, until it's ready, we could move Matt into the guest room," Amy suggested.

"I think that's a good plan." Miles turned to Natalie and Jana. "What about you two? Do you still want to share a room, or do you want your own bedrooms?"

The girls looked at each other, and then Natalie threw her arms around Jana. "We want to share," she said.

"You understand the room won't belong to just you, right?" Miles asked.

Natalie nodded. "It'll be ours." She grabbed Jana's hand and pulled her to her feet. "Let's take your dolls to our bedroom."

"Okay." Jana, all smiles, grabbed her box of dolls, and she and Natalie started to climb the stairs, Scrappy behind them.

"Do you like this plan, Matt?" Amy asked.

He nodded. "I think it'll be awesome to sleep in the attic."

"Can I choose the color of my walls?" Colton asked. "I want them to be black."

"Hmm," Amy said with a wrinkle of her nose. "Not black—but maybe a dark blue."

Colton didn't look at Amy but continued to stare at Miles as if he hadn't heard her and was waiting for his dad to weigh in.

"Amy answered your question, Colton," Miles said.

He pressed his lips together and then said, "She's not my mom."

It felt like a slap to Amy's face, and she had to take a deep breath.

"No," Miles said calmly and evenly, though Amy could sense his underlying frustration. "She's not your mom, Colton, but soon she's going to be my wife and your stepmother, and with that will come the authority to make decisions for you. I'm giving Amy full permission to be your other parent, and I expect you to respect and honor her."

Colton continued to stare at Miles, and then he turned and went up the stairs again, this time disappearing into the hallway above.

It was just Matt sitting there, his eyes wide as he looked at Miles and Amy.

"Matt," Miles said, "why don't you take your things up to the guest room and start making yourself at home. Let the other kids know that your mom and I are going to keep bringing things into the house."

"Okay." Matt jumped up, grabbed his box, and climbed the stairs.

Miles faced Amy, a sad smile on his face.

"I'm sorry, Amy."

She took another deep breath and let it out. "You don't need to apologize for Colton. I know this is hard on him. His attitude isn't your fault."

"Why don't we step outside and get a breath of fresh air?" Miles put his arm around her shoulders and drew her along with him.

She willingly followed, snuggling into his warm and steady presence.

They walked out onto the porch, and Amy took a breath of the cold, crisp air. She was thankful for the stillness of the winter evening.

"Are you okay?" Miles asked.

"Yeah. I spend all day with first graders. I have a thick skin."

"I know you do, but Colton is going to be your stepson soon, and you don't get to send him home at the end of the day. You get to *come* home with him."

Amy smiled. "I know. He's only speaking out of fear and hurt. I'm sure he wishes that his mom was here instead of me."

Miles shook his head. "I know Shelby loves her children, but she wasn't a good fit as their mom. She even admitted it herself."

Shelby, Miles's ex-wife, had left four years ago when Colton was seven and Natalie only three. She went to Paris and remarried, terminating all her parental rights. She called on occasion and sent a card at birthdays, but that was the extent of her involvement in their lives.

"I know," Amy said as she leaned against the railing and crossed her arms. "But he can't possibly understand that right now. It'll take him some time to get used to the idea that he's going to have another parent."

Miles joined her. There was just enough light coming out of the house to see him. He was so handsome, with dark brown eyes and salt-and-pepper hair. But his good looks were only a small part of his charm. Miles was compassionate, intelligent, thoughtful, and loving. As a physician, he was well respected and successful. To know that he loved her was the greatest gift anyone had ever given Amy, and she knew he felt the same way about her.

"We got through this with Jana," he said. "This isn't a one-and-done deal, I think. We're going to probably have more talks in the future about adjustments, especially as we navigate having four teenagers in the house at the same time."

Amy rolled her eyes. "And now I'm terrified." She laughed.

Taking her hand, Miles smiled at her. "You're incredible, Amy. I'm so thankful for you. I know that you're going to do a wonderful job bringing our families together."

She looked up at him and met his smile. "I won't be doing it alone."

He was about to kiss her when a loud sound came from the neighboring house.

"Dr. Anderson!" a woman called as she shuffled along her sidewalk. "I want to have a word with you."

Miles groaned.

"What is it?" Amy asked quietly.

"It's not what, but who. Beverly Brady."

"You don't sound excited."

"Wait and see why." He took her hand again as they walked off the porch and met the neighbor on the boundary of their properties.

Beverly Brady was probably in her early sixties, a good ten years older than Miles and Amy. She wore expensive-looking jewelry and a pair of slacks that were sharply creased down the middle of each leg. Thick perfume emanated off her, and she held a small white dog in the crook of her arm.

"Beverly," Miles said, "I've been meaning to introduce you to my fiancée, Amy Allen."

"Mrs. Brady will do," Beverly said as she nodded at Amy. "I've seen you around, and I've seen your children." She pursed her lips. "Far too much, if you ask me."

Amy frowned. What was that supposed to mean?

"What can I do for you?" Miles asked.

Beverly sighed, a long, laborious sound. "I don't know how many times I have to address the same issue with you, Dr. Anderson."

"Miles, please," he said.

"Dr. Anderson," she said again, pointedly. "Until you and your children moved into this neighborhood, it was a very quiet, peaceful place to live. Since then, I've had very little peace and quiet to call my own. Moppet barks incessantly when they are playing outside." She petted the dog in her arms. "And if that wasn't hard enough to deal with, I can hear the children's shrieks and shouts at all hours of the day. It sends my hair on end every single time."

"I've spoken to them many times—"

"They have trampled through my yard again," she interrupted. She pointed to a spot on the front corner of her property. "You can't see it in the dark, but there are children's footprints in my yard. It's quite obvious with the snow. I know it's them."

"I'm sorry."

"You must tell them not to touch my property. I cannot have them getting hurt or hurting something of mine. I take great pride in my lawn."

"I know you do." Miles sounded like it was taking a lot of effort to stay pleasant.

"Of course, it's not so obvious in the winter. But under the snow are dormant plants and flowers that cannot be disturbed. You do understand, don't you? My yard is my pride and joy."

"Yes, of course."

Beverly looked at Amy in the dim light. "And you have two children as well."

"I do."

"What a shame." Beverly sighed again. "Two more children to make noise and drive my little Moppet to distraction. I've had to put her on a sedative to deal with the anxiety the children cause her. Extra children mean extra opportunity to disrupt the peace and quiet and destroy my beautiful yard."

"I'll speak to them," Amy said. "And we'll do our best to keep the children away from your yard."

"Your best probably won't be good enough," Beverly said, "but I suppose it's all I can expect."

Amy glanced at Miles, taken aback by this woman's behavior. Was she really this cantankerous?

"Have you already moved in?" Beverly asked with raised brows.

"No. We're getting married in three weeks. The children and I will move in then."

"More's the pity." Beverly continued to pet Moppet. "As soon as I heard Dr. Anderson was getting married, I had to investigate you."

"Investigate me?"

"I can't have just anyone living next door to me."

"Excuse me," Miles said, "but I don't think it's up to you to decide who I marry and ask to live with me, Mrs. Brady."

"Of course it's not up to me, but it would be foolish not to know my neighbors. I investigated you before you moved in too, Dr. Anderson."

"Mrs. Brady," Miles said, his patience dimming, "I believe this conversation is over. We will do our best to keep the children out of your yard, but beyond that, we can't control their voices when they're playing outside. There's nothing more to discuss."

Beverly stood straighter and lifted her nose. "We'll see about that."

"Are you threatening us?" Amy asked.

"Threatening you?" She scoffed. "That question is beneath me."

And with that final statement hanging in the air, Beverly turned on her heel and walked back to her house.

"See," Miles said. "That's why I wasn't excited to talk to her. She's not an easy person to deal with."

"It's unfortunate that she's not willing to be pleasant. Kindness goes a long way, especially between neighbors."

Miles put his arm around Amy and led her toward their cars where there were boxes to be unloaded.

"Let's forget about Beverly and focus on us," he said. "This is a happy time in our lives, and we need to count our blessings."

Amy smiled up at him. "You're at the top of my list."

He kissed her. "And you're at the top of mine."

Amy was content to forget about Beverly and the wedding veil and the fast-approaching closing date and even the fact that someone had tried to sabotage their wedding. But it wasn't so easy to forget about Colton's unhappiness. The children and Miles were the most important part of her life, and as long as she kept that in focus, she could get through the rest of it.

She hoped.

Chapter Four

Tuesday afternoon was cold, but the bright January sunshine warmed Amy as she sat inside Miles's Jeep, waiting for their appointed meeting time with the director of the Museum of Wonders. After school, Amy had dropped the kids off at Tracy and Jeff's house, and then Miles had come by to pick her and Tracy up to go to the museum. Jeff had agreed to keep an eye on the kids, but they were pretty self-sufficient and were given instructions to get their homework done before playing for the afternoon. No doubt Jeff would have a special project for them to work on. He liked to tinker around with woodwork, and the kids often came home with birdhouses or other things they made in his garage.

"Any luck finding out who canceled all your vendors and booked them for herself?" Tracy asked from the back of Miles's Jeep.

"I haven't had a chance to call anyone." Amy glanced at the clock and saw they had fifteen minutes before their appointed meeting. And since the parking lot was empty, they hadn't even tried to knock on the museum door. It was usually closed midweek during the winter, and the director was meeting them for a special tour. "I guess I could call one of them now."

"Which one do you know the best?" Miles asked. "Maybe they'd be most likely to tell you who took your spot."

Amy thought through the list of vendors. "Probably Kristen, the photographer. She took a portrait of the kids and me last summer. She was so awesome to work with, and her prices are reasonable." Amy felt the keen disappointment all over again. "I was really looking forward to having her photograph our wedding."

Amy searched for Kristen's number on her website. "Here goes nothing." She pressed the call button and put her phone on speaker so Tracy and Miles could hear the conversation.

"Kristen Morgan photography," Kristen said when she answered. "How can I help you?"

"Hi, Kristen, this is Amy Allen calling again."

"Oh hi, Amy. I'm still so sorry about what happened."

"I know. So am I." Amy tried not to let her disappointment influence her words. "I'm actually calling because after I spoke to you, I found out that all of my vendors had been canceled and rebooked by someone else."

"All of them?"

"Yes. The reception hall, caterer, everyone."

"I can't believe it. That's horrible."

"I agree. And it can't be a coincidence. Someone systematically called around and said they were me and canceled my wedding plans. I'm literally starting at the beginning, and my wedding is only three weeks away."

"I've never had this happen before, Amy. I'm so sorry. What can I do to help?"

"I'd really like to know who canceled everything. I can't necessarily prove that it's the same person who then booked my vendors, but if the same bride took all my slots, it would be pretty obvious."

"You'd like to know who booked me for January 27th?"

"Yes, please."

"Do you plan to contact her?"

"I would like to talk to her, at the very least."

There was hesitation on the other end of the phone. "I don't like to give out personal information about my clients, especially if they might get a harassing call from the person I shared their name with."

"I'm not going to harass her," Amy said, a little offended. "I just want to talk to her. I think I have a right to know who canceled all my vendors, don't I? It was an underhanded trick, and now I'm the one left scrambling to pull a wedding together."

Again, Kristen paused. Finally, she let out a short breath. "Her name is Mercy Fellbaum—but that's all the information I'm willing to give you."

Mercy Fellbaum. Amy looked at Miles and then Tracy to see if they recognized the name, but both shook their heads. Amy didn't know the name either.

"Thank you, Kristen. I promise I won't harass her. I just need to know if she's the one who canceled my wedding."

"Okay. Good luck finding new vendors."

"Thanks," Amy said, though the response was a little dry. She wished Kristen would call Mercy and tell her that she knew what she'd done and that she wasn't willing to photograph her wedding anymore. But Amy understood that Kristen couldn't come out and accuse Mercy. Maybe Mercy was an innocent bystander.

After Amy ended the call, Tracy asked, "Is there anyone else you can talk to? If Mercy is the one who booked your florist and baker and wedding hall, then it's probably a good bet that she's the one who canceled all of them too."

Amy thought for a second. "Maybe I can call Trish again. She's the first one who told me what happened. She seemed really nice and apologetic."

Amy found the number she had called the day before.

The phone rang only once, and then Trish answered. "Hello, this is Trish."

"Hi, Trish. It's Amy Allen calling again."

"Oh hi, Amy. What can I do for you?"

"After we spoke on the phone yesterday, I called my other vendors and found out that they'd all been canceled."

"Really?" Trish's voice held surprise. "That's unbelievable."

"I'm hoping you might answer a couple of questions for me."

"Sure. If I can."

"I'm wondering if the woman who called and canceled my order sounded like me."

"It's hard to say. You and I only spoke a couple of times, and when the call came to cancel your order, I was so disappointed I wasn't really paying attention to the voice."

"But it was a woman about my age, do you think?"

"Yeah."

At least that narrowed down the suspects somewhat. But it still left a lot of possibilities.

"Is it possible to let me know who booked my slot?"

Trish hesitated much like Kristen had.

"I know this puts you in a tough spot," Amy said. "And I promise I won't harass your customer, but I need to know if this was done by the same person."

"I guess it won't hurt. Let me pull up the information so I don't get it wrong."

Amy glanced at Miles and Tracy, and they both gave her encouraging smiles.

"Her name is Mercy Fellbaum," Trish said after a moment.

Amy sucked in a breath, because even though she suspected this had been intentional, she was still surprised.

"That's the name of the woman who booked my photographer," she said. "And I have a feeling she booked all my other vendors too."

"That's so strange," Trish said. "I wonder why she did that."

"Because she wanted the best, and I already had all the best booked."

"That's sweet of you to say."

"Is there any way you'd consider turning Mercy down and honoring the order I placed?" Amy asked, hopeful.

There was a pause, and then Trish said, "You know what, I am going to do that. You're not to blame here, and you shouldn't have to suffer. I'll call Mercy today and let her know that I can't bake her wedding cake."

Amy glanced up at Miles, and he grinned at her.

"Thank you," Amy said, excitement and relief flooding her. "You don't know how much of a burden this takes off me."

"You're welcome. And good luck with the other vendors. I hope all of them will do the same."

Before Amy hung up, she asked for the gluten-free cupcakes that had prompted her call the day before, and then she said goodbye.

After she disconnected, Miles said. "That's great. I'm so happy we have the cake order restored."

"I'm so relieved." Amy leaned her head back on the seat. "I was really excited about the cake Trish was going to make—*is* going to make. It'll be beautiful."

"We still have a little time," Miles said. "Why not call the wedding hall and the caterer you had planned to use and see if Mercy booked them too. Maybe they'll honor their first commitment to you."

Amy did just that. First, she called Gather, the wedding venue she had originally booked for the reception. But the manager was not willing to give her any information about who had booked the building for that day. Though, when Amy asked if it was a woman named Mercy Fellbaum, there was a telltale pause before he said he wasn't at liberty to say. And he wouldn't hear of canceling on his client and letting Amy take the spot again.

After she hung up, disappointed, she called the caterer, but it was more of the same. She wouldn't share any information and wouldn't honor Amy's original order.

When she hung up, feeling deflated, another car pulled into the parking lot.

"That's Elaine," Tracy said.

Elaine Hartford was the director of the Museum of Wonder and one of Tracy's friends.

Miles, Tracy, and Amy stepped out of the Jeep. Miles and Elaine had never met, so Tracy introduced them, and then they approached the brick building.

The Museum of Wonders had opened a year and a half ago. The building had once been a factory, but it had been turned into a beautiful cultural epicenter with artifacts from around the world.

"I can't believe I've never been here," Miles said after Elaine opened the front door and invited them to enter.

The ceilings were impossibly high, and pedestal columns circled the main room. Metal-framed, industrial windows let in a ton of light and allowed them a spectacular view of the tree-lined street outside. Unique treasures from Ancient Egypt, Greece, India, and more filled the room.

"Thank you for meeting with us," Amy said to Elaine.

"Tracy explained what happened with your wedding venue," Elaine said. "I'm so sorry. I hope you find the culprit."

"I have an idea who it might be." Amy paused. "Do you know anyone named Mercy Fellbaum?"

Elaine shook her head. "I can't say that I do."

After Elaine showed them around, they sat down at her desk to chat about the possibility of using the museum for the wedding reception.

"You're the first couple to ask about renting the museum," Elaine said with a smile. "So I spoke to my board of directors and asked them what they thought about the possibility. After a lot of discussion, we agreed it would be a wonderful opportunity for the museum."

Amy smiled at Miles, who took her hand.

"We still need to put some policies in place," Elaine continued, "but I don't think that will prevent us from solidifying your plans today, if you're interested."

"I think we are." Amy looked at Miles, and he nodded.

"Great."

As Elaine pulled out a calendar to check the date, Amy felt another piece of the puzzle slip into place.

This hadn't been her original choice, but she loved that they would be the first couple to use the museum for their wedding reception. It would be unique and special for them and for their guests.

For the first time, there was a part of Amy that was happy that this had happened. If it hadn't, they wouldn't have considered the museum for their reception.

Maybe the rest of her plans would be better in the long run. She could only hope.

But it still didn't answer her pressing question. Why would a stranger try to sabotage her wedding? Was it purely selfish? Or did Mercy have another reason?

Amy was determined to find some answers.

"Do you like the museum?" Miles asked Amy as they climbed back into the Jeep.

"I love it. Do you?"

"I do too." He smiled at her. "I think it will be a really classy and unique place to have a reception."

"I think so too." Amy turned to Tracy. "Thanks for the suggestion."

"You're welcome. And speaking of suggestions, do you two have a minute to stop at the historical society? I'd like to pop in and ask

Tawny if she remembers Grandma Pearl loaning the wedding veil to them for some reason."

"I don't mind," Miles said.

The plan was to leave the kids with Jeff for the evening and head back to Amy's house to keep packing. A little detour to the historical society wouldn't take long, since it was close.

"I'll wait in the Jeep while you all run in," Miles said as he pulled up to the front door to drop them off. "Take your time."

Amy and Tracy walked up the short sidewalk. The historical society was housed inside the local county museum, near the banks of the Mississippi River in downtown Canton. The building was on one level and shaped like a U with a gazebo in the courtyard, overlooking the river.

Tawny Hagstrom was the curator of the museum and knew more about Canton history than anyone else Amy knew. She often helped Tracy, Amy, and Robin solve mysteries they found in Grandma Pearl's attic. For years, she had been begging them to donate their grandmother's diaries to the historical society, but they had resisted. Grandma's journals were priceless heirlooms for their family.

"Hello," Tawny said as soon as she saw Amy and Tracy enter the building. "My two favorite sisters."

Amy smiled and leaned against the front counter. "Hi, Tawny."

"What can I do for you today?" Tawny asked them. "Unless you just stopped by to say hi."

"We did stop by to say hi," Tracy said, "but we have a question too."

"Good. I like questions." Tawny pushed her designer-framed glasses up the bridge of her nose and waited.

"This might be a long shot," Tracy began, "but we went into Grandma's attic to look for our family's wedding veil, and we can't find it. The veil was first worn by our great-grandma in 1921 and then by our grandma and other brides in our family. Amy was hoping to wear it at the end of the month in her own wedding, but when we went to get it, it wasn't there."

"We can't think of any reason why it would be missing," Amy added, "unless Grandma Pearl loaned it to someone. We don't think she would have loaned it to another bride, since it's a family heirloom, so the only other thing we could think of was that she loaned it to the historical society."

"Hmm." Tawny frowned. "When was the last time you saw it?"

"Six years ago, at Sara's wedding," Tracy said. "She was the last bride to wear it."

"So it had to have gone missing sometime in the past six years?"

"Yes." Amy nodded.

"We've definitely had a lot of events in the past six years that involve historical clothing," Tawny said. "And your grandma was always eager to share whatever she could. I don't specifically remember a wedding veil…" She paused and squinted, as if thinking hard. "Wait. I do remember hosting a wedding expo here about five years ago. We had a fashion show, highlighting wedding attire through the years. There were so many people in and out of here that weekend, and we borrowed a lot items." Tawny pulled out a piece of paper and scribbled a note. "I'll do some checking. There are a few board members and volunteers who were involved back then that I haven't spoken to in a while, so it might take some time to call around. But I'll see what I can find."

"Thank you so much," Amy said, feeling another boost of hope. "We appreciate your help."

"Of course. If it was on loan to the museum, we need to make sure we get it returned to you."

"And," Tracy added, "there's less than three weeks before the wedding, so it needs to be soon."

"I'm sorry if this was our fault," Tawny said.

"Right now, it's only a possibility," Tracy assured her. "No one is guilty of anything."

"I just hope there wasn't an accident, or something like that." Tawny shook her head. "Or that someone stole it. There could be several reasons why it wasn't returned to your grandmother, I'm afraid."

"We'll cross that bridge if and when we get to it," Amy told her. "Let's not jump to any conclusions."

"I'm on it, ladies. I'll make this a top priority."

"Thanks, Tawny." Amy smiled at her.

"Anytime. And if you need help with anything else, let me know."

"I actually do have another question," Amy said. "I'm not sure if you can answer it, but it doesn't hurt to ask, does it?"

"Of course not." Tawny waited.

"Do you happen to know someone by the name of Mercy Fellbaum?"

"I do." Tawny nodded. "Why?"

"We think she's the person who called Amy's vendors and canceled them." Tracy explained to Tawny what had happened.

"That's hard to believe," Tawny said, looking truly surprised. "I've gotten to know Mercy a little at church, and she's a sweetheart."

"She goes to your church?" Amy asked.

"Yes. She just moved to Canton this past summer, because her fiancé lives here. He's a machinist for Charles Industries. I can't imagine her being mean or vindictive."

"Why would she cancel all my wedding vendors?" Amy asked. "And then book them for herself?"

Tawny shrugged. "I have no idea. That doesn't sound like Mercy at all. But I guess I could be wrong. Maybe there's a side to her that she doesn't show us at church."

"Do you know where she lives or works?" Tracy asked. "We would really like to talk to her."

"She works at Whimsy, the new gift shop in town. I'm sure she'd be happy to talk to you—she's so friendly. I know you'll think so too. I just can't picture her doing something like that. Maybe she's a victim in this situation too."

Amy wasn't sure how that could be, but she was willing to consider the possibility. She trusted Tawny. If Tawny said Mercy Fellbaum was a sweet woman, then she probably was. But there still had to be a good explanation for all of this.

"Thank you for the information," Amy said. "I'll stop by and chat with Mercy and see how this happened. Maybe she was just in the right place at the right time to snatch up my wedding vendors, but it does seem fishy, doesn't it?"

"Yes, extremely fishy." Tawny nodded. "But I'm sure Mercy will accommodate you as much as she can."

After saying goodbye, Tracy and Amy left the museum and went back to Miles's Jeep.

"Any luck?" he asked.

"Tawny is checking on the wedding veil," Amy told him. "Grandma Pearl might have loaned the veil to the museum for a wedding expo five years ago. Maybe it was put into storage at the museum or into someone's closet by accident, and since Grandma passed away, no one thought to ask about it until now."

"I sure hope we can find it," Miles said. "I know how much it means to you."

"Same here. But that's not the big news. Tawny also knows Mercy Fellbaum."

"Really?"

Amy told him what Tawny had shared with her and Tracy.

"Do you want to stop at Whimsy now?" Miles asked.

Glancing at the clock, Amy saw it was just past five. "The shop is probably closed for the day, and we really need to head back to my place and tackle another room or two this evening. We only have a week and a half before the closing."

"Okay." Miles pulled out of the parking lot and onto the main road, heading toward Amy's house.

"I can stop by Whimsy tomorrow after work with you," Tracy volunteered. "It might be easier to confront Mercy with someone at your side."

"Thanks. Let's plan on that." Amy could call Whimsy, but it would be better to talk to Mercy face-to-face.

For now, though, Amy didn't have the energy to think about her encounter with Mercy. She was thankful they had a baker on board and even more thankful for a reception venue, though they still needed a photographer, a caterer, and a florist. Plus, they would need to send out a change of address to all their guests. Thankfully, the church was still theirs for the ceremony, and when the guests arrived they could inform them of the address change, but just in case, Amy would send out a card in the mail too.

Another thing on her ever-growing to-do list. Made longer by Mercy Fellbaum's machinations.

Chapter Five

As soon as the trio returned to Amy's house, they got busy packing up the living room and dining room. Those would be the easiest rooms to finish and the least disruptive for the family's daily life over the next week and a half.

"Any luck finding the wedding binder?" Tracy asked Amy a couple of hours later as she stacked another box on top of the ones waiting by the back door to go to Miles's house.

"No." Amy frowned and pushed away a tendril of brown hair that tickled her nose. "I've looked high and low for it, both here and at school. I can't find it anywhere."

Tracy leaned her elbow on the top of the box. "Do you think someone stole it?"

"From where? Did someone come into my house and steal it? I highly doubt it."

"Did you have it out in public with you?"

Amy thought hard for a moment. "I did have it at the coffee shop last week when I stopped in. But I'm almost positive I had it when I left."

"Do you remember having it since then?"

"I honestly don't. That might have been the last time I used it. I thought I brought it home and put it on my desk, but I suppose I could have accidentally left it there."

"I would think someone would have called you from the coffee shop if they had found it," Tracy said. "Which leads me to believe that maybe it was stolen."

"By who?"

"Mercy, maybe?" Tracy shrugged. "It might be how she got all the information about your vendors."

"But why?" Amy asked. "Why would she want to sabotage my wedding?"

"I don't know. But there has to be a reason. Maybe it was purely selfish and she was just stealing all the vendors for herself."

"I guess I can ask her about it tomorrow when we meet her, but I doubt she'll be honest with me if she took it."

"It could be one explanation though." Tracy stood straight. "It's a large, three-ring binder. It can't simply disappear."

Amy nodded, but she hated to think that someone would purposely steal the binder from her—even if that person hadn't tried to ruin her wedding on purpose.

"I'm going to start packing up the kitchen," Tracy said. "I'll leave a few pots and pans for the next week and a half, but you and the kids will eat from paper plates, right?"

"I think that'll be the easiest."

"Perfect." Tracy took an empty cardboard box and went to Amy's cabinets and started to pack.

Miles entered the house. "My Jeep is almost full," he said to Amy. "I don't know how many more boxes I'll be able to pack in there. I'll probably need you to drive Colton and Natalie home from Jeff and Tracy's house."

"Or, we could make a quick stop at your house to drop things off before we go and pick up the kids," Amy said. "We should let Scrappy out too. It's been a long day in his crate."

"I let him out on my lunch break."

"Good." Amy looked at her watch and noticed how late it was. The kids would need to be picked up soon to get ready for bed.

"We should get going then, if we're going to make the stop."

Amy nodded and then called to Tracy. "Are you going to stay for a little longer? It's getting late, and Miles and I are going to stop by his house to drop off everything before we pick up the kids."

"I'll keep working here," Tracy called back.

"Thanks." Amy put on her coat as Miles took a couple of the boxes and headed outside.

After Amy grabbed her keys and purse, she lifted another box and left the house.

"Let me take it," Miles said as he met her on the sidewalk.

"I hate moving." Amy released her burden to him.

"Thankfully, it'll be the last time." Miles smiled at her and gave her a kiss.

Amy returned the smile and went to get into her car.

A few minutes later they pulled into the driveway at Miles's house. It was dark outside, and there wasn't a single light on inside.

The temperature was dropping, and Amy could see her breath as she got out of the car and started to unload the back seat.

"Looks like we'll be getting snow overnight," Miles said when he met her at her car and took a couple of boxes. "They're predicting a few inches."

"Ugh. It'll make moving even harder." She couldn't wait until the move was over and the wedding was behind them and they could settle into daily life.

Miles unlocked the back door, which led into the kitchen, and flipped on the light. Scrappy started to bark from his crate in the corner.

"I'll never get tired of walking into this house," Amy said with a happy sigh. "So many good memories here."

"And many more to come," Miles said.

Amy had spent a lot of time at Miles's house while they were dating in high school. Though there had been some updates, it looked almost the same as it had over thirty years ago.

They set the boxes in the corner of the large kitchen, and then Miles went to get another load while Amy let Scrappy out the door.

Ten minutes later, after they had brought in the last box, fed Scrappy, and returned him to his crate for a little while longer, Amy started to walk to the back door to leave.

"Just a minute," Miles said. He took something off the island and held it in his hand. "I've been meaning to give this to you, but I kept forgetting."

Amy waited for him, not sure what he had picked up.

Miles stopped in front of her, his dark brown eyes full of something sweet and gentle. "I had thought about making a big deal of this gift, maybe giving it to you when we went out to eat, or in an elaborate gift box. But"—he took Amy's hand in his—"I decided that it didn't need to be marked by a special occasion. Just giving it to you would be special enough."

"What is it?" Amy asked, tilting her eyebrows in curiosity.

Miles opened Amy's hand and laid something cool and small on her palm. "I'm giving you my home."

The key to Miles's house was in her hand. But he wasn't just giving her a key to the building and the contents within. More than that, he was giving her and her children a place to belong.

Unexpected tears came to Amy's eyes, and she had to blink them away. "Thank you," she whispered.

"I want you to feel free to come and go as you please." He drew her into his arms. "You don't need to tell me that you're coming and going. You don't need my permission. I want you to feel at home here, Amy, just as you would at your house. I was serious when I told the kids yesterday that this isn't just my home anymore. It's ours. You and the kids are giving up a lot to move in here, and I want you to know how much I appreciate your sacrifice."

Amy reached up and wrapped her arms around him in a tight hug. "And I know how much you're sacrificing to welcome three more people into your house. Thank you, Miles."

He held her close for a long time, and when she finally broke their embrace, she had to wipe away more tears. But there was also a smile on her face. "We should probably go pick up the kids."

"I wish we were bringing them back here together," he said as he flipped off the kitchen light and followed her out the door. "I can't wait until we're all living in the same house."

Amy nodded in agreement. The wedding couldn't come soon enough, though there was so much to do beforehand, it was hard to focus on the excitement of the coming event without the anxiety of everything leading up to it.

The next day, Miles picked the kids up from school to take them to his house to haul boxes to the attic. After that job was done, they would head over to meet Amy and Tracy at Amy's house for more packing.

In the meantime, Amy and Tracy would go to Whimsy and meet Mercy Fellbaum in person.

"I'm nervous," Amy said as she and Tracy drove toward Whimsy.

"What do you have to be nervous about?" Tracy asked. "Mercy is the one who's guilty. Not you."

"I know, but what if I make the accusations and she denies them?"

"Of course she's going to deny them," Tracy said. "What we need to do is try to figure out if she's lying or telling the truth when she denies them."

"That's what makes me nervous—trying to figure it out. I hate confrontation."

"I can do most of the talking if you don't want to."

"No." Amy took a deep breath as Whimsy came within sight. "I need to do this. It's my wedding I'm fighting for."

"Just know I'm here for you."

"I do."

Amy pulled into the parking lot and found a space to park her car. She looked at the building for a second, trying to pull her thoughts together.

"Ready?" Tracy asked.

"No, but I'm going to do it anyway."

The snow had started to fall overnight, and it was still coming down. Thankfully, the walkway into the store had been shoveled, but it was still slippery as they made their way into the gift shop.

Warmth and the smell of fragrant candles greeted them the minute they entered the store. Whimsy was full of beautiful home decor, household items, greeting cards, and more. A large wall clock instantly caught Amy's eye. It was made of dark, polished wood, and had ornate metal numbers. Despite Amy's nerves, she could envision the clock on the wall leading up the main staircase at Miles's home—her home.

There were a few other shoppers meandering through the store as Amy and Tracy walked to the checkout counter. Behind it was a woman unpackaging little figurines. She glanced up and smiled.

"Welcome to Whimsy," the woman said. "I'm Pammy, the owner. Can I help you find something today?"

Amy nodded. "I'd like to speak to Mercy Fellbaum, if she's here."

"Of course." Pammy motioned to the corner of the store. "I think she's working on a display over there."

"Thank you." Amy and Tracy moved in the direction Pammy had pointed.

"We need to come back, just to shop," Tracy said quietly as they walked down an aisle of wall hangings. "There are so many cute things in here. I wish you would have let us throw you a bridal shower."

"We don't need a thing," Amy protested. "We're combining two houses. Bridal showers are for people just starting out."

"I know," Tracy said. "But it would be fun to have something for the new house, wouldn't it?"

Amy looked at the wall clock again, and Tracy followed her gaze. "Wow. That's beautiful."

"I was thinking it would look nice on the staircase wall at Miles's house."

"It would!" Tracy's voice filled with excitement. "You have to let me buy it for you, Amy."

"No."

"Yes." Tracy nodded. "I'm going to get it for you in lieu of a bridal shower."

"It's probably expensive."

"I don't care. It isn't every day my little sister gets married."

Amy knew that tone in Tracy's voice. She wasn't going to be easily dissuaded.

They turned the corner and found a young woman working on a display. A long, narrow dresser sat in the middle and was covered with candlesticks, books, vases, greenery, and more. It was beautiful and made it obvious that the young woman was a talented decorator.

She looked up at them and smiled. Her name tag said MERCY.

"Hello," she said.

"Hi," Amy and Tracy replied at the same time.

"Can I help you find something special, or are you just browsing? We're having a sale on our candles today. Buy one, get one half off."

"We're not here to buy candles," Amy said as she crossed and uncrossed her arms, suddenly not sure what to do with them. "We actually came to talk to you."

"Oh?" Mercy's eyebrows rose high in surprise. "What can I do for you?"

Amy cleared her throat, unsure how to approach the issue. She decided to just jump in. "I'm getting married on the twenty-seventh of this month."

Mercy smiled, looking amazed and pleased. "I'm getting married on the twenty-seventh too."

"I know." Amy glanced at Tracy, and she nodded for Amy to continue. "I recently learned that all of my wedding vendors were canceled by someone who claimed to be me."

Mercy frowned but didn't say anything.

"And when I tried to rebook them," Amy continued, "they told me that someone else had already taken my spot—and that someone was you."

"Oh, goodness," Mercy said, her troubled blue eyes glancing from Amy to Tracy and back again. "I'm so sorry. I had no idea."

"You had no idea that Amy's plans had been canceled when you booked her vendors?" Tracy asked with a frown.

"No." Mercy shook her head. If she was pretending or lying, she was doing a believable job of it. She looked genuinely shocked and surprised by Amy's news. "My fiancé and I have been engaged for almost a year, and I moved to Canton to be near him last summer. We didn't have a wedding date settled, but we recently learned that he's being sent to Japan for his job in February and he'll be gone for four months. We want to be married before he leaves, so we decided to pull the wedding together as quickly as we can. I spoke to several friends and my fiancé's family and asked for their suggestions for wedding vendors. I started calling the ones at the top of the list and found that all of them were free." She studied Amy, her eyes wide with regret. "I'm so sorry this happened. I had no idea. What can I do to help?"

Amy glanced at Tracy again. Was Mercy being honest?

The look on Tracy's face told Amy that she didn't know either.

"At this point," Amy said, "I have a new reception venue selected, so that isn't a problem anymore."

Realization dawned on Mercy's face. "Is that why Trish called me from Cake Creations and said she couldn't make my cake?"

Amy nodded, feeling a little guilty, though she didn't know why. It might have been easier to feel justified in her anger if Mercy had been difficult.

Mercy worried her bottom lip and looked down at the floor. "I'm not from around here, so I'm not sure who I can call about a cake, but I'm planning to search online after work. I'm sure there's someone else." She looked up again, her gaze troubled. "I suppose I can cancel the caterer and photographer and the florist and figure out something else. After all, it's only right. They were yours first."

"That won't be necessary," Amy found herself saying. Clearly, Mercy was at a loss. If she was being honest, and this was all a big mistake, then she wasn't to blame. She shouldn't have to change her plans too.

"I'm going to call Les Trois Colombes," Amy said. "It's a French restaurant here in town. They were my second choice for caterer. And the florist said that she might be able to sneak both of us into her schedule if she can find help that day. If not, there are other florists nearby who can help me. And my cousin knows a good photographer we can use."

"I'm so sorry," Mercy said again. "What a horrible thing to happen just before your wedding." She paused. "I didn't catch your name."

"Amy Allen," Amy said, "and this is my sister, Tracy Doyle."

"It's nice to meet you both," Mercy said. "Though I wish we had met under different circumstances. I hope you'll let me know if there's anything I can do to help you."

Amy nodded. "I will." She felt a little shaky, as if she had worked herself up for a big battle but was now deflated because she didn't know who her enemy was.

"Can I get your number?" Mercy asked. "I'll call you if something comes up or if I hear anything about who might have called the vendors and canceled your plans."

They exchanged numbers, and then Amy and Tracy walked away.

"Well," Tracy said as she maneuvered toward the large clock on the back wall. "Do you think she's innocent?"

Amy took a deep breath. "I have no idea. She's sweet—just like Tawny said—and she seemed to be surprised. I would think she's innocent if it wasn't such a coincidence that someone called to cancel my vendors and then Mercy happened to book all of them right after."

"I agree. But she might be telling the truth."

"That doesn't change the fact that someone canceled my plans."

"Right, and we should keep her in mind, but we need to branch out and consider other possibilities."

"Like who?"

"We still haven't found your wedding binder. Maybe we go back to the coffee shop and check there."

"There's too much to do today. I'll have to go some other time."

"Okay, but for now we're buying that clock and taking it to your new house."

"I don't know. Maybe I should run it by Miles."

"He gave you the key to the house and told you it's your home now, right?"

"Yes," Amy said slowly.

"Then treat it like that, Amy. I know Miles wouldn't mind if you brought a new clock into the house. And it would look great on that wall. He'll love it. Besides, it's a gift. You can't say no to a gift, especially one from your older sister."

The closer they came to the clock, the more Amy liked it.

"It's perfect," Tracy said. "Please let me buy it for you."

It didn't take much to convince Amy, and ten minutes later, they walked out of Whimsy with an oversized clock that would hang on the wall in her new home.

Chapter Six

Instead of turning right to go to her house from Whimsy, Amy turned left to head toward Miles's house.

"This feels so weird," she said as she glanced in the rearview mirror and saw the large clock in the back seat. "In all the years I've known Miles and been to his house, I've never been there by myself."

Tracy smiled. "I remember how much time you spent there in high school. Did you ever imagine it would be your house one day?"

"No." Amy shook her head. "Even when I thought about the possibility of marrying Miles back then, I imagined us living somewhere outside of Canton." Amy had been eager to leave Canton behind and explore the world after high school. It was one of the reasons she had broken up with Miles. Her friends had convinced her that she needed to be free and single when she went to college. But it hadn't taken long for her to realize that she had made a mistake. She had wanted to talk to Miles, but she had hurt him and never felt right about contacting him afterward. His life had taken a different path in Connecticut, and she had gone her own way. But God, in His infinitely perfect timing, had brought them back to Canton and into each other's lives.

"His parents are really excited for us," Amy continued, thinking about the last call they'd shared. "They love knowing the old house will be so full again."

Amy had always gotten along with Miles's family. Mimi and Clarence, his mom and dad, were thrilled when they heard that Amy and Miles were dating again, and happier still when they announced their engagement. Miles's older brothers lived out of state but would come for the wedding with their families. Mimi and Clarence planned to come to town a few days early to help with last-minute plans and to host the rehearsal dinner the night before the wedding.

It had been so long since Amy's parents had passed away in a car accident, the thought of having a mother-in-law and father-in-law filled her heart to overflowing. The Andersons had already embraced Matt and Jana as their own and told the kids to call them Grammy and Gramps, like the other grandkids did.

Amy pulled into the driveway and parked her car near the back door. Beverly Brady was on her stoop watching Moppet do her business. She glanced up at Amy and Tracy as they got out of the car.

"Miss Allen," Beverly called as she came down her steps and scooped Moppet into her arms. "I'd like a word with you."

"Ugh," Amy said.

"Is this the neighbor you told me about?" Tracy whispered as they walked toward the property line.

"Yes. Unfortunately."

"Just smile," Tracy said.

Amy tossed a cheesy smile at her sister.

"Miss Allen." Beverly stopped at the property line and waved at them, as if they hadn't already seen her and were walking in her direction. "There are more footprints in my yard. You said that you were going to talk to the children."

"Hello, Mrs. Brady," Amy said. "This is my sister, Tracy Doyle."

Beverly glanced briefly at Tracy, as if she was of little consequence. "Did you speak to the children?"

"I did."

"Ah." Beverly lifted her chin, as if she suddenly put all the pieces of a puzzle together. "Then that means you don't have them under control. I suspected as much. There's nothing worse than disobedient children. I can't abide it."

"All children are disobedient from time to time," Amy said, trying to remain calm. "But I don't believe the children did it on purpose. I'll talk to them again."

"Talk, talk, talk," Beverly mocked. "What they need are consequences and discipline, not more talking."

"They are my children," Amy said in an even voice. "I will decide how to parent them."

"I knew this was going to be a nightmare when I heard Dr. Anderson was getting married. Not to mention now there's a puppy that barks and growls at my Moppet." Beverly petted Moppet's head. "I'll never have another moment of peace. I'd stop the wedding if I could."

Amy's jaw dropped at Beverly's audacity. "I'm sorry you feel that way," she said, "but I believe this conversation is over. We are getting married and moving into the house. If you don't like it, then perhaps you should think of moving."

Tracy made a soft noise, as if she was surprised at Amy's statement, but didn't say anything as Beverly turned away and stormed into her house in a huff.

"Wow," Tracy said. "I rarely hear you lose your cool."

"She's set out to dislike the children and me without even knowing us. We don't need that kind of negativity in our lives, especially right now." Amy's frustration level had escalated but not just because of Beverly Brady. She felt like everything was piling on top of her, squeezing out more of her energy, patience, and time.

They turned toward Amy's car, and Amy opened the back door to get the clock.

"What if Beverly is the one who tried to sabotage your wedding?" Tracy asked as she helped Amy with the clock. "She just said that she'd stop it if she could. Maybe she tried."

Amy paused as she glanced at Beverly's house. Could her new neighbor be the culprit?

"Do you honestly think she thought she could stop the wedding by canceling our vendors?" Amy frowned. "Surely she knew we would find other vendors."

"Maybe she didn't expect you to call all the vendors ahead of time to confirm. Maybe she thought you'd get to the day of the wedding and that's when you would realize you didn't have anything in place."

"If that's the case, then she's even meaner than I thought," Amy said as she closed the car door.

She and Tracy shuffled toward the house with the clock. Amy had the house key on her keychain, so she had to set her end of the clock down to unlock the door.

"I'm not going to lie," she said with a smile. "I've always loved this house. It's exciting to have a key to it."

Amy opened the door and then picked up her end of the clock. They stepped into the kitchen with the sound of Scrappy's greeting barks, and Tracy closed the door behind her.

"Just a minute, Scrappy," Amy said as they slipped off their shoes. "I'll get to you as soon as I can." They walked into the butler's pantry and through to the dining room. "I still feel weird being here without Miles."

"You might for a while, but it will eventually feel like home."

Everything was quiet and still as they entered the hallway.

"How will we hang it up there?" Amy asked. They set the clock down and looked up at the high wall.

"Hmm." Tracy pursed her lips. "We'll need a ladder and some screws, and we'll need to find the studs. This is a heavy clock."

"This is probably a job for Miles," Amy said. "I don't even know where to look for a ladder and tools."

A noise at the back of the house made the ladies pause as Scrappy started to bark again.

"What was that?" Amy whispered.

"It sounds like someone just came into the house." Tracy peeked around the side of the staircase toward the dining room.

Amy's heart started to pound hard. "Did someone follow us in?"

She knew it was an irrational thought, but what if Beverly had come in? What if she was so upset, she meant to hurt them?

"Should we slip out the front door?" Tracy asked. "Or wait to see who it is?"

"I don't know." Amy looked around for a possible weapon, but there wasn't anything in sight that would work against an intruder.

There was more commotion, and voices started to drift out to them from the kitchen. Excited, energetic voices.

"Those are the kids," Amy said. Her shoulders relaxed.

A second later, the door between the dining room and the butler's pantry flew open and Natalie and Jana appeared.

"Hi, Mom!" Jana said with a toothless grin.

"Hi." Amy's heart started to return to its regular rhythm, but as soon as she saw Miles come through the door, a surprised look on his face, a new feeling surfaced.

She felt like an intruder.

"Hey," Miles said. "This is a nice surprise. I didn't know you and Tracy were stopping by here."

"I—I hope it's okay."

"Of course it's okay." Miles gave her a quick kiss and teased her with his smile. "I told you last night you should come and go as you like."

"I know, but—"

"No buts, Amy." He winked at her.

"Tracy bought us a gift." Amy moved aside and showed him the clock. "We thought it would go really nice on the staircase wall."

She could see in his gaze that he knew she was trying to explain herself, and he shook his head. "It's okay, Amy. I promise. And I really like the clock—I think it will look great on the wall. Thank you, Tracy."

"You're welcome," Tracy said.

Amy turned to Miles. "What are you guys up to?"

"The kids and I stopped for an after-school scoop of ice cream, so we're just getting here to let Scrappy out and move the boxes up to the attic. Do you want me to help you hang the clock while we're here?"

"I'd love that. Thank you."

"I'll go grab a ladder from the garage and get some screws and a stud finder. I'll be back." Miles walked back toward the kitchen, calling out directions to the kids to start hauling the boxes from the kitchen to the attic. He took Scrappy out with him.

"See," Tracy said, smiling, "he loves the clock."

"Ow!" came a cry from the kitchen. "Colton dropped a box on my foot!" Jana yelled.

"I'm not carrying your dumb boxes up to the attic," Amy heard Colton say. "You do it."

"Daddy said we should all do it," Natalie said. "Help us, Colton."

"These aren't my boxes."

"Come on," Matt said. "Let's just get it done."

"You do it," Colton repeated. "I don't want all this stuff in my house anyway."

Amy sighed. She had hoped that their talk with the kids the other night had made an impact on everyone—especially Colton. But it sounded like things weren't resolved yet.

"Don't worry about the kids," Tracy said to Amy.

"They're fighting all the time now."

"Just like siblings?" Tracy asked with a knowing smile.

Amy sighed again. "I suppose."

"It's only natural that they're going to fight more, since they're together more. And with all the changes going on, I'm sure they're feeling their own levels of anxiety. They just don't have the skills yet to deal with it like adults."

"I know some adults that don't know how to deal with their anxiety either."

"True. So give the kids some grace. It'll get bet—"

"Ow!" Jana cried again. "Don't push me, Colton!"

"You're in my way. I'll push you if I want to push you. This is my house."

Amy couldn't wait for them to resolve the issue on their own. "I'll be right back," she said to Tracy and left to join the children in the kitchen.

As soon as she walked through the door, Jana looked up at her, tears in her eyes.

"Colton pushed me," she said.

"You're a baby," Colton told her. "It didn't hurt."

"Yes it did!"

"Kids," Amy said as she put up her hands to quiet them, "everyone needs to calm down."

"Colton started it," Matt told Amy. "He dropped the box on Jana's foot on purpose, and then he pushed her. And he won't help us like Miles said."

"Colton, is that true?" Amy asked. Though she had heard the progression of the fight from the other room, she wanted him to have the opportunity to explain himself.

"She started it," Colton said. "She's the one moving all her stuff in here."

Amy took a deep breath. "We talked about this, Colton—"

"I don't want any of you here," he said, his cheeks red with anger. "I wish you weren't marrying my dad!" He turned and stormed out of the kitchen and up the stairs, stomping all the way.

"Colton!" Amy called out after him. "Colton, come back here."

He didn't listen to her, and a few seconds later she heard a door slam shut.

"What's going on in here?" Miles came through the back door with Scrappy at his heels. "I could hear the yelling all the way outside."

Matt's, Jana's, and Natalie's eyes were huge as they stared at Amy. Jana's tears slid down her cheeks.

"The kids were fighting," Amy said, trying not to get emotional about what Colton had said. "Apparently, Colton dropped a box on Jana's foot and then pushed her."

"And," Natalie explained, "he told Amy that he didn't want any of them living here. He said he doesn't want you to get married." She leaned forward and whispered, "I think he stole your wedding binder too."

Amy met Miles's disappointed gaze.

Miles shook his head. "I'm sorry, Amy. Colton's behavior is totally unacceptable. I'll talk to him."

"Should we talk to him together?" Amy asked.

"I don't think that's a good idea." Miles crossed the kitchen and put his hand on her arm. "He'll probably shut down if you walk into his room with me. I think it's time that he and I have a heart-to-heart."

Amy nodded. "You know him better than I do. But let me know if you need me."

He gave her arm a gentle squeeze and then left them in the kitchen.

Jana approached Amy and gave her a hug. Natalie joined her.

"I want you to live here," Natalie said, looking up at Amy with a smile. "I can't wait until you're my mom too."

Amy's heart expanded, and she bent to give Natalie a big hug. It was the first time Natalie had said something about Amy's new role in her life. "Thank you, sweetie. I can't wait to be your mom."

"Can I call you Mom?" Natalie asked. "Like Jana does?"

Miles had told Amy that Natalie was so young when her mother left them that she didn't have any memories of her. Would that make it easier for Natalie to accept Amy as her new mom?

"Of course," Amy said. "If you'd like to."

Natalie nodded, a big smile on her face.

It felt like a win to Amy, though Colton's attitude—and Natalie's claim that he stole the binder—dimmed the moment. Had he stolen the binder? And, if so, was he responsible for all the vendors canceling?

It wasn't possible—was it?

Chapter Seven

By Friday, Amy was as close to burnout as she had ever been. It took all her energy and focus to get through the school day. Fridays were often hard because her students were eager for their weekend break and had been cooped up in the classroom all week. But with Amy's stress and workload, her patience was thin. She hadn't had a minute to herself all week and didn't see any time for relaxation for the next two weeks until after the wedding. She and Miles planned to get away to neighboring Quincy, Illinois, for two nights after the wedding, for a mini-honeymoon, but the amount of work to do beforehand was daunting.

"I should have never agreed to sell the house on such short notice," Amy said to Tracy as they drove to the grocery store for more boxes that afternoon. "This whole thing is madness. I'm so overwhelmed, I broke one of my own rules in class today and raised my voice at the kids."

"It won't be much longer," Tracy reassured her. "We're over halfway through the house."

"We haven't moved any of the large furniture yet. That'll be the hardest."

"We'll get Jeff and Terry over to do the heavy lifting. It shouldn't take much time at all. Have you decided what to do with it?"

"I hope we can sell most of it, but I haven't had time to take pictures and put them online." It was yet one more thing to add to her growing to-do list. "I feel like every time I accomplish something, there's five more things I need to get done."

"Did you ever line up a florist?"

"Yes. Thankfully, the florist I had booked was able to get some help. She said she could pull off Mercy's wedding flowers and mine."

"And the caterer?"

"Miles and I will be going to Les Trois Colombes on Tuesday for a food tasting. I have to decide which options I'd like served at the reception. And," she added, "I need to get the change of address cards in the mail as soon as possible. I printed them off last night, but I need to stuff them in envelopes and put address labels on them."

"The kids could do that with Jeff," Tracy volunteered. "He's looking for a project to do with them tonight."

The kids would be at Tracy and Jeff's house again as Tracy, Miles, and Amy did more packing. Robin planned to be over that evening too.

"You don't think he'd mind?"

"No. I think he'd like to be helpful."

Amy's shoulders lowered in relief. "That would take a lot off my plate. I need to buy stamps when we're at the grocery store too. Don't let me forget."

As soon as one thing was eased from her mind, another one popped up. She needed to remember to go to the post office at some point for a change of address form and to call all her utilities to cancel them.

"Just breathe," Tracy said. "I know this is all a lot. But we're here to help. You shouldn't be afraid to ask for what you need."

"You're already helping as much as you possibly can."

"I can do more. All you have to do is ask. All my kids are out of the house, and it's just Jeff and me. Sure, I work part-time, but I don't have nearly as much to do as you in a given day."

"I appreciate the offer." But even as Amy said it, she knew she wouldn't ask Tracy to do any more for her. She and Miles had made the choice to get married and to close on her house in two weeks. Why should Tracy need to be put out because of their choices?

They arrived at the store and entered the building. Soon, Amy had boxes and stamps. They also picked up a frozen lasagna to put into the oven for supper, and a bag of salad mixings.

When they were back in the car, Tracy asked, "Have things gotten any better with Colton?"

Amy sighed and looked out the drivers' side window for a moment before she started the car. "No. Miles's talk with him didn't go as well as he or I would have liked. Colton is still giving us attitude anytime we ask for his help or talk about the wedding and the move."

"It might take some time."

"That's what you keep saying."

"Because it's true. Colton probably has more memories of his mother, which makes it harder for him to accept you than Natalie. Now that the wedding is around the corner, it might be getting too real for him that he's going to have a new mom."

Amy nodded. "I know you're right. I just wish I knew how to get through to him."

"Time will build his trust. Be consistent and loving. He'll come around."

"I hope so, because it could be very unpleasant living in the same house with someone who doesn't want us there."

"Did you ask him about the wedding binder?"

"Yes, but he said he didn't take it."

They drove to Amy's house, and Miles was already there, hauling boxes to his Jeep. He waved at them on his way back to the house.

"Just remember the most important thing," Tracy said to Amy as they pulled into her garage. "Your relationship with Miles. The kids will eventually grow up and move out of the house, but you and Miles will always have each other. As you work through Colton's problems, don't lose sight of the reason you and Miles are getting married. Your love for one another and your desire to share a life together far outweigh the difficulties life will throw at you."

"Thank you, Tracy." Amy smiled at her sister. "I'm so grateful for your advice and wisdom."

Miles appeared at the open door of the garage as Amy and Tracy got out of the car.

"Do you need help unloading the boxes?" he asked.

"Yes. You're just in time." Amy gave him a quick kiss and then opened the trunk. "We took all we could fit."

"Hopefully this will be the last run for boxes," Miles said as he started to remove them from the trunk. "We're getting close."

"I haven't even started on my room," Amy said. "I'll need to pack bags for the kids and me to use at Tracy's for a week and then send the rest of our stuff to your house. I've been putting it off as long as I can so we don't have to live out of suitcases at home."

They left the garage and went into the house. There, Amy gathered all the supplies for Jeff and the kids to send out the change of address mailing.

"I'll run these over to my house," Tracy said to Amy. "Robin will probably be here by the time I get back. Then we can tackle the bedrooms. Maybe we'll find that wedding binder yet."

Amy couldn't help but wonder if Colton had lied about taking the wedding binder. Was he hoping to delay or cancel the wedding? She didn't want to make more ripples by asking him about it again. They had enough tension between them without her accusations.

"Okay." Amy nodded. "I'll see you in a bit."

Tracy left Amy's house just as Miles reentered with another load of empty boxes from the store.

"Alone again," Miles said with a wink and a smile at Amy. He set down the boxes and then put his arms around her. "I'm going to like when this is all over and we can have more of these quiet moments together."

Amy returned the embrace. "What makes you think we'll find quiet moments with four children in the house?"

"We'll find a way. They have to go to sleep, don't they? Even if our quiet moments are only an hour before bed, I'll take it. But I plan to date you, even after we're married."

"Oh, you do?" Amy lifted her eyebrows with a smile. "Do you have something specific in mind?"

"I was thinking we should establish a weekly date night—and keep it, no matter what happens. We can go out to eat or see a movie. Take the boat out in the summer or go cross-country skiing in the winter. Anything that gives us an excuse to spend time together—alone—without any interruptions."

Amy took a deep breath. "Just thinking about it eases my burdens right now."

"I wish I could do more to ease your burdens."

"You are." Amy put her hand on his cheek. "You're doing as much as me."

He shook his head. "I'm trying to keep up, but you're dealing with all the little details, like sending out the change of address mailing and managing the chaos of selling your house. I'd like to do more."

"We'll get through this," Amy said, trying to reassure herself just as much as him. "Only another week until we close on the house and the papers are signed. Then we can turn all our attention to the wedding. After that, we can settle into the house and figure out the rest."

"Like why Colton's attitude has changed so much over the last couple of weeks."

Amy looked at the buttons on Miles's shirt, trying not to meet his gaze, afraid he'd see the hurt she felt at Colton's attitude.

Miles placed his fingers under her chin and lifted it. "I know it's bothering you a lot, Amy. You don't have to hide it from me. I don't want to keep anything secret or hidden between us."

"I keep thinking about Natalie's accusation. Do you think Colton took the binder? Do you think he had anything to do with canceling the vendors?"

"Wasn't it a woman who made the calls?"

"I suppose. But maybe he got a friend to do it for him—a girl who sounds older."

"I don't think he would do something like that." But the look in Miles's eyes told Amy he wasn't certain. "Maybe it's time for another family meeting. Let's take tomorrow evening off and have a game and pizza night at home. It might be as simple as relieving some of the stress and anxiety and letting the kids talk freely about their feelings. We can ask Colton about the binder then."

Apprehension filled Amy's chest at the thought of taking the evening off when they still had so much to do, but Miles was right. They needed to de-stress and let the kids know that they weren't being lost in the shuffle and busyness of the move and the wedding. As hard as it would be, she knew it was the right thing to do. "I think that's a good idea."

"Me too." Miles kissed her and held her.

It felt good to just stand in his embrace, but all too soon, Robin was at the door, calling out her arrival. And it was time to get back to work.

"Wow," Robin said a few minutes later as she looked around Amy's house. "You guys have made great progress. The house is starting to echo."

"Most of the main floor is packed," Amy said as she walked Robin into the living room. "We'll start on the bedrooms today. The furniture will be the last to go. I'm still trying to figure out what to do with the stuff we aren't taking to Miles's house."

"You have time."

"I like your confidence."

"Point me in the direction you'd like me to go, and I'll get to work."

"Let's start in Jana's bedroom," Amy suggested.

They took a few empty boxes and went upstairs. Amy grabbed a suitcase to sort out the things Jana would need for the week they stayed at Tracy's house.

"Any news about the veil?" Robin asked as she opened Jana's dresser and began to remove the clothing inside.

"Nothing yet. I was hoping Tawny would call or text with some news by now. To be honest, I haven't really thought much about the veil the past few days, things have been so hectic around here."

"I don't blame you. I remember planning my wedding and getting ready to move in with Terry. It was probably the most stressful time of my life, and I wasn't a mom yet."

"I wish it didn't have to be this way. It's supposed to be a happy, joyful occasion."

"It is. But I think we set our expectations so high, and then nothing can measure up to it, and that's where a lot of the disappointment and stress comes from."

Amy thought about her wedding plans and had to admit that Robin was right. She'd had such high hopes for her wedding, and now that most of the plans had changed, she struggled to be as excited.

"I'm so frustrated with myself," Amy said as she placed a few pairs of pants into Jana's suitcase. "I know the most important thing to focus on is that at the end of the day, Miles and I will be married. It shouldn't be about the wedding."

"Right," Robin said slowly, "but you can't deny that the wedding is important. It's a big day, and rightfully so. There's nothing wrong with wanting it to be beautiful and special, but we need to adjust our expectations and be able to pivot, if needed. You've done that already. Just keep in mind you might need to keep doing it. Ultimately, the wedding will be wonderful and you'll look back at it with good memories, if you're willing to go with the flow."

Amy nodded. "That's easier said than done."

"Always."

They worked for another thirty minutes before Tracy appeared at Jana's bedroom door.

"I just got a text from Tawny," she said, holding up her phone. "She thinks she found something helpful with the veil."

"Oh?" Amy stopped putting Jana's books in the box she was packing. "What did she say?"

"She asked if we had time to run over to the historical society. She wants to show us something. If you and Miles want to go and get a little break, Robin and I can stay here and keep packing."

"I couldn't ask you—"

"You didn't, Amy." Tracy interrupted Amy's protest. "I made the offer. You and Miles need a little time to yourselves, and we've got this under control. Right, Robin?"

"Absolutely."

"If you want to stop and get coffee afterwards," Tracy suggested, "you should do that too. Take your time and just enjoy each other for a few minutes. Okay?"

"Are you sure?" Amy asked.

"Yes."

Amy hugged her sister and her cousin and then went downstairs to find Miles. He was washing the windows in the living room.

"Hey," she said to him, feeling lighter than she had in a week. "Want to go on a little date with me right now?"

He turned to her, a smile on his handsome face. "Always."

"Don't you want to know what we're going to do?"

"It doesn't matter."

Amy grinned and motioned for him to follow her. "Tawny wants us to stop at the historical society to check out something she found, and then we're going to get some coffee. It was Tracy's suggestion. She and Robin will stay here and keep packing."

"You don't have to ask twice. We can drop off another load at the house while we're out. My Jeep is packed tight."

They were soon in Miles's Jeep, pulling into the historical society parking lot. It was only open for another twenty minutes by the time they walked in the front door.

"There you are," Tawny said. "I was hoping you'd get here before I left."

"Tracy said you had something to show us."

"I do." Tawny pulled a gray archival box off her desk and placed it on the front counter. "I found some pictures and want you to take a look at them."

Amy and Miles stood on the opposite side of the counter and watched as Tawny removed some pictures from the box.

"These were taken at the event we held five years ago. They're pictures of our models wearing historical bridal clothing. I thought you could see if you recognize your family's veil."

Amy glanced at the photos and immediately recognized the veil on one of the models. "That's it, right there."

"Are you sure?" Tawny asked.

"Yes. I'd know it anywhere."

"Good. I've been having a hard time tracking down the people who were involved in this event, and those I have don't know anything about the veil. I wanted to make sure it had been on loan to the historical society before I kept looking. That's why I thought about these pictures. I have one more person I've been trying to get ahold of, but she's in Arizona for the winter and hasn't returned my messages."

"Thank you so much for all your help," Amy said. "This means a lot to me."

"I'm happy to do it. I just wish I'd had more luck by now. The wedding is two weeks from tomorrow, right?"

Amy nodded.

Tawny returned the pictures to the box. "Did you get a chance to meet Mercy?"

"I did." Amy glanced at Miles before looking back at Tawny. "She said she doesn't know anything about the vendors being canceled. She was very sweet, like you said."

"She doesn't have much family in the area—just her fiancé's aunt, so she's gotten very close to several of us at church. We're her surrogate family, in a way."

"She mentioned that she called all the vendors that her fiancé's family suggested. I assumed there were several family members."

"No, just her fiancé's aunt, Beverly Brady."

Amy raised her eyebrows and glanced back at Miles. He seemed just as surprised as she was.

"Beverly Brady?" Amy asked.

"Yes. Do you know her?"

"She's my neighbor," Miles said. "And she doesn't like us very much."

"Really?" Tawny frowned. "I can't imagine someone not liking you two. Why does she feel that way?"

"She thinks the kids are too loud and disruptive." Amy shook her head, stunned that Beverly was related to Mercy—or at least that she would be soon. "I still can't believe that Mercy and Beverly know each other."

"Small towns are funny that way." Tawny shrugged. "It seems like everyone is related to everyone else."

"But this one is a little too coincidental," Miles said. "Just yesterday, Beverly told Amy she would stop our wedding if she could."

"Do you think it was Beverly who canceled our vendors?" Amy asked him. "Maybe she did it for Mercy and Mercy lied to us."

"I can't imagine Mercy lying to you," Tawny said. "But I don't really know Beverly, so I can't vouch for her."

"Hmm." Amy nibbled her bottom lip as she thought about Beverly. Was she capable of doing something so underhanded out of spite?

Amy had a sneaking suspicion that she was.

Chapter Eight

$\mathscr{B}$y Saturday evening, Amy was relieved that she and Miles had agreed to take the night off to spend it with the kids. They had made a big push that morning and afternoon at her house and finished packing up the bedrooms, and then they had taken the kids back to Miles's house to relax. As Amy and Miles prepared supper, the kids were scattered throughout the house. Natalie and Jana played with Scrappy in their room, Matt was settling into the guest room, and Colton was watching a movie in the family room. Amy was sad that Colton was excluding Matt, since they had worked so hard on their friendship in the early months. But Colton wanted his own space, and Amy had talked to Matt about offering it to him.

All that was left to pack and move out of Amy's house were the bathrooms and the large furniture, but Amy was ready to let it rest for a couple of days and worry about the furniture later.

"I've never worked so hard in my life," she said as she pulled plates and napkins out of the cabinet in Miles's kitchen. The smell of pizza permeated the air and made her stomach growl.

"I think the hardest part is behind us." Miles set the two boxes of pizza on the counter and then moved to the refrigerator where he grabbed the chocolate milk.

"I hope so. I'd hate to think the hardest part is ahead of us." Amy smiled as her gaze landed outside the window and in the backyard of Beverly Brady. Beverly was sweeping the freshly fallen snow off her back stoop while Moppet sniffed around her bushes.

"Does Beverly live alone?" Amy asked.

She and Miles hadn't had a chance to talk much about the connection between Mercy and Beverly, but they had the time now.

"As far as I know. I never see anyone else leave or enter her house, unless she has guests over."

"It's an awfully big house for one woman and her dog."

Miles came to the window to look out with Amy. "One of the other neighbors told me that her husband passed away right before I moved in. She has five or six children, but none of them live in the area, and they rarely come home to visit her."

"How sad. She must be lonely."

Miles put his arms around Amy from behind. "The neighbor did say that she's gotten harder to get along with since her husband died." He rested his chin on her head. "Sometimes I feel selfish for how much I have."

"It's not selfishness to be grateful for your blessings or to enjoy what God has given you. But we need to remember to share what we have with others. I just wish Beverly would let us into her life. She's been so standoffish to all of us. If she would open up and be kind, we could offer her our friendship. She's obviously grieving."

"Maybe we offer it anyway. Make a concentrated effort to invite her over, stop to say hi when we see her in her yard, and offer as much kindness and hospitality as we can."

"Do you think she's the one who canceled all our vendors?" Amy asked, turning in his arms to look at him.

"I don't know why she would."

"To try to stop our wedding and help Mercy."

Miles sighed. "I think we should give Beverly the benefit of the doubt."

"If it wasn't Beverly or Mercy, who would have done that to us?"

"Are you still worried it was Colton?"

Amy shook her head as her shoulders came up in a shrug. "I don't know. I hope not. I'd like to think not. But he hasn't been happy with any of us lately. Maybe he thought he could stop it from happening if he had everything canceled."

"Well," Miles said as he let Amy go, "there's one way to find out." He took her hand. "Let's go have a talk with him before supper."

"You don't think he'll be upset that you've brought me into it?"

"He might be. But he needs to get used to it, Amy. From now on, we're a team. You and me. There might be times when the kids need our one-on-one attention, but there are other times when they need both of us. And, right now, I think Colton needs to see that we're a united front. I know he's upset, but we have to let him know that everything is going to be okay."

Amy nodded and took a deep breath to prepare herself for this conversation. She followed Miles out of the kitchen, wondering why she felt so nervous to talk to an eleven-year-old boy.

And then it struck her. She wanted Colton to love her, to accept her, and to be pleased with his father's choice in a wife. It was important that Colton and Natalie approve of her. But, if she couldn't get Colton's approval, she needed to find a way to be okay with that.

The television was in the family room, where there was comfortable seating and a basket of throw blankets perfect for a winter night like this one. The original fireplace had been converted to gas at some point, so it was easy to turn on with a flick of a switch.

As Amy and Miles entered the room, they found Colton lying on the couch, a blanket on his legs, and the fireplace pushing heat into the room. He was watching men doing trick shots and basketball drills.

"Hey, buddy," Miles said when Colton glanced up at them. "Can you pause the TV for a second? Amy and I would like to talk to you."

Colton was a miniature version of his father and reminded Amy a lot of Miles when he was younger. But Miles had always been a happy-go-lucky kid. Colton was moody and often brooding when he was unhappy. And lately, that had been often.

"Do I have a choice?" Colton asked with a scowl.

Miles shook his head and lifted the remote to pause the screen. "Go ahead and sit up, Son."

Colton pulled himself to a sitting position, but he still slumped on the couch and crossed his arms.

Amy took a seat next to Miles on the other sofa, willing to let him lead this conversation.

"Amy and I know you're unhappy about the wedding and having her and Matt and Jana move in."

Colton stared at him but didn't respond.

"You also know that we already talked about this—on a couple of different occasions—but we're not seeing any progress in your attitude, and that's concerning us." Miles leaned forward and put his elbows on his knees. "I've said a lot of things over the past couple of weeks, but you've been really quiet. Amy and I are here to let you tell us what you're thinking and feeling."

Colton glanced at Amy, and she saw the hurt and fear hiding behind his anger.

"You can be honest with us, Colton," she said as she too leaned forward. "There's nothing you can say that will make us stop loving you. If you're angry, tell us you're angry. If you're afraid, then tell us. We want to help make this change in your life as easy as possible."

"I don't want you to move in," Colton said, tears coming to his eyes. "I don't want you to be my dad's new wife."

Amy nodded, but didn't speak, hoping he'd continue.

When he didn't, Miles asked gently, "Why not, Colton?"

Colton wiped at his face to remove the tears. "If you're married and have two more kids, you won't have any time for me. We won't play basketball or go fishing or do any of the things we used to do together. You'll be with Amy, or you'll be helping Matt. I won't be your only son anymore."

Miles moved off the couch and sat next to Colton. He put his arm around him, and Colton laid his head on Miles's shoulder.

"Did you know that I have room in my heart—and my life—for all the people I love?" Miles said. "When you start to care for someone new, it doesn't push out the other people you love. Your heart only grows bigger. That's why families are so special. The more people you have in a family, the more love you have. I'm not going to pretend that things won't be different, but different isn't always a bad thing, Colton. It can mean that when we play basketball, you and Matt can team up on me and maybe beat me once in a while."

A small smile tilted up Colton's lips.

"And when we fish, there'll be another person fishing with us. Maybe we'll bring home more to eat." Miles glanced up at Amy. "Amy and I know how important it is to have special one-on-one time with our kids. There will still be times when it's just the two of us. Because no matter what happens, I'll always and forever be your dad. Whether you like it or not."

Colton buried his head in his dad's chest and wrapped his arms around him. "I like it—a lot."

"So do I, buddy," Miles said as he hugged Colton. "And I know it's going to take some getting used to, but I promise that our family will be stronger and better when we add Amy, Matt, and Jana. Our love for each other will grow and grow and grow, and one day, you'll wonder how we ever lived without them in our lives."

Amy's heart warmed, listening to Miles speak to his son. She had never doubted saying yes to his marriage proposal, but in this moment, she was more convinced than ever that it was the best decision she had ever made. Miles was a truly good man, with a big heart. She couldn't imagine joining her life to anyone else.

Colton pulled back from his dad and wiped at his cheeks again. He glanced up at Amy, remorse on his face. "I'm sorry for being mean to you and Matt and Jana. I felt awful when I was doing it."

She left her couch and sat on the other side of him so she could give him a hug too. "It's okay," she whispered. "I forgive you."

Colton dropped his gaze to his lap. "I took something from you."

Amy looked at Miles over Colton's head.

"Was it my wedding binder?" she asked.

Colton nodded. "I took it from your house when we were there one time. I thought if you didn't have the binder, maybe you couldn't plan the wedding."

"Did you have someone call the vendors from Amy's list?" Miles asked, keeping his voice even.

Colton shook his head. "No. I just kept the book under my bed. I didn't even open it."

"Can you get it for me, please?" Amy asked.

With a quick nod, Colton stood and left the family room.

"At least now I know who took the binder," Amy said with a sigh. "But it doesn't answer my other questions."

"I'm just happy he confessed without us interrogating him."

"That's because you're a good dad and he trusts you," Amy said with a smile. "The way you parent is very special, Miles. I know I have a lot to learn from you."

He held out his hand to her, and she took it. "You amaze me all the time, Amy. I think we have a lot to learn from each other."

She squeezed his hand, but her mind churned with questions. She wanted to know who canceled her wedding vendors, if for no other reason than to hold them accountable.

Was it Mercy? Beverly? Someone else? Amy was determined to find out.

"Sundays are my favorite day of the whole week," Natalie said as she stood in Grandma Pearl's attic with Amy, Tracy, Robin, and Jana the next day.

"Why is that?" Amy asked.

"Because we get to come to Aunt Tracy's house," Natalie said matter-of-factly, as if she shouldn't have had to explain herself.

Amy shared a smile with both Tracy and Robin.

"I love having little girls in the attic again," Tracy said as she opened an old bureau. "Grandma Pearl grew up here, then Aunt Ruth, and then came me, Amy, and Robin. After us, Sara played up here, and now you two are here."

"Someday our daughters will play here too," Jana said, lifting the wide skirt of one of Tracy's old prom dresses that the girls were playing dress-up in.

"I can't wait," Tracy said. She closed the bureau with a sigh.

"It's not in there either?" Robin asked.

"Nope. Any luck for you, Amy?"

"No." Amy stacked the boxes she had just gone through. "If that veil was up here, I think we would have found it by now."

"I think I might have found something," Robin said. She brought an old shoebox over to Amy and Tracy. "There are a bunch of newspaper clippings in here, and one of them is about the bridal show they had five years ago. It looks like they interviewed Grandma Pearl about her veil. She must have clipped out the article to save it."

"There's even a picture of her with it," Amy said with a surprised smile.

Robin took out the clipping and set the box aside as Tracy and Amy stood on either side of her to read the article.

"She gave the family history of the veil," Tracy said. "And now I know why I don't remember this. Look at the date of the article.

That's the summer Jeff and I traveled for a month following the Liberty Trail in South Carolina."

"I'm happy that Grandma thought to save the article," Robin said. "But I'd be surprised if she hadn't."

Just one glance around the attic was a reminder that Grandma Pearl saved everything.

"Look at this," Amy said, pointing to the bottom of the article. "It says that all the historical clothing would be on display through the month of June under the care of Nora Tanner, an intern from the University of Missouri specializing in textile archivism. I wonder if Tawny has contacted Nora to see if she knows where the veil is."

"It's worth checking into." Tracy pulled out her cell phone. Within minutes, she had a text sent off to Tawny.

"I think we've looked up here about as much as we can," Amy said.

"My stomach is growling," Robin added. "Let's get some lunch and ask if Tawny can locate the intern to see if she knows where the veil went."

"Sounds good to me," Tracy said. "Lunch should be about ready." She motioned to the girls. "Are you hungry?"

"Yes!" they both cried.

Amy and Tracy helped the girls out of the dresses and hung them in their plastic bags again before they all went downstairs.

As the girls ran ahead, down the steps and through the bedroom, Robin said, "Were you able to connect with my friend about photographing your wedding?"

"Yes." Amy nodded. "I have spoken to her, and she's available on the twenty-seventh. Thanks for connecting us. She sent me a link to her website, and I was able to see her work. It's beautiful. And because she's never photographed a wedding before, she's willing to do it for free. Of course we'll offer to pay her again, but she was pretty adamant that she doesn't want to charge us."

"Wow," Tracy said. "Another hidden blessing amidst all this trouble."

"I'm definitely trying to find the silver linings where I can," Amy said.

"Have you discovered anything else about Mercy?" Tracy asked as they walked out of the room and into the upper hallway.

"No more than what Tawny said, that Mercy and Beverly are related," Amy said. "But I haven't been able to speak to either one of them about it. And I haven't had much time to seek them out."

"Maybe you should visit with Beverly," Robin suggested. "Ask her if she knows anything about the cancelations."

"I can imagine how well that conversation will go." Amy put her phone in her pocket. "But it's worth trying. I'm already disappointed in how our relationship has started, but if she's the one who canceled my vendors so her nephew's bride could take my spots, then she needs to be held accountable."

"I agree." Tracy led the way down the steps to the entry and then through to the back of the house where the men were getting lunch on the table. Miles and Terry set the table and filled glasses with water while Jeff took a large pan out of the oven.

"That smells delicious," Amy said, taking a deep whiff. "I don't think I've ever had baked spaghetti before."

"It's an old family recipe," Jeff said. "I thought it would be a nice change from lasagna."

"I can't wait to give it a try."

Tracy pulled her phone out of her pocket and read something on the screen before saying, "Tawny just responded. She said that she had forgotten about Nora Tanner working at the museum and that she would try to find contact information for her. She'll let us know if she gets ahold of her and what she has to say about the veil."

"That's good to hear," Amy said, though she couldn't deny the disappointment that grew inside her. "I'm starting to think that I need to come up with a backup plan for a veil. If we can't find the family one in time."

Tracy and Robin nodded their agreement though they both looked disappointed too.

It would be a shame not to have the veil for her wedding, but Amy was running out of time and clues to find it.

Once again, she had to remind herself that at the end of the day, the only thing that mattered was marrying Miles.

Chapter Nine

I think this is the best use of the space," Amy said to Miles as they stood in Natalie and Jana's bedroom later that afternoon, setting up bunk beds. The room was a good size, but the beds would allow for more floor space.

"I love our bunk beds," Jana said in a serious voice. She sat on the floor with Scrappy asleep on her lap. "It's almost like a castle."

The bunk beds were white with steps on the end to get to the upper bed. Amy had purchased matching pink bedspreads for the girls, which was what they wanted.

"It's harder to put together than I anticipated," Miles admitted as he used a screwdriver to attach two pieces.

"You're doing good, Daddy," Natalie said with a nod.

The girls anxiously waited for the beds to be complete while the boys played outside. There wasn't much daylight left, but they had been eager to build a snow fort in the backyard. Amy and Miles were happy to see them getting along. And Amy was thankful she had the wedding binder in her possession again.

"We'll take turns sleeping on the top bunk," Natalie told Jana. "But I'll sleep up there until you move in."

"That's not fair," Jana said with a frown. "I want to sleep up there too."

"You can," Natalie assured her. "But not for two more weeks."

Jana turned to Amy, a disgruntled look on her face. "That's not fair, Mama."

"I'm sorry," Amy said. "But we aren't moving in here until after the wedding, and that's thirteen days away. It'll go by fast, and then you'll get to be here all the time."

"I want to sleep here tonight," Jana said. "Can I?"

"You have school in the morning," Amy reminded her.

"So does Natalie," Jana said.

Miles glanced up from the instructions. "Jana can stay over," he said. "I'll make sure she gets to school in the morning. I have some extra toothbrushes, and most of her clothes are here already."

Natalie and Jana looked at Amy with pleading eyes, and she couldn't think of a single reason to say no. "I guess it'll be all right."

The words were barely out of her mouth before the girls started to cheer and wake up Scrappy. The three of them ran around the room with excitement.

Miles smiled at Amy. "I hope they feel this way after living together for a couple of months."

Jana hugged Natalie and said, "I'll always feel this way about Natalie."

Natalie grinned and hugged her back.

"Mom!" Matt's anxious voice rang through the house. "Mom!"

"Dad!" Colton yelled in an equally troubled voice.

Amy glanced at Miles, and she saw concern in his face.

"We're in the girls' room," Amy called. "What's wrong?"

The boys ran up the stairs and slid to a halt in the doorway, both of them talking at once.

"I didn't mean to do it," Colton said.

"It was my fault too," Matt added. "I grabbed Colton's hockey stick, and he pulled it back."

"She's really mad," Colton added. "She said she's calling the police."

"What are you talking about?" Miles asked. "And only one of you talk at once. What happened?"

The boys' cheeks were pink from the cold and their excitement. Their eyes were bright and full of worry. Both were breathing heavily.

"We were playing hockey in the driveway," Colton said, "and Matt grabbed my stick, so I couldn't hit the puck into my goal. I got the stick loose and then I hit the puck as hard as I could. It missed the goal and hit Mrs. Brady's colorful window and broke it."

"Her stained-glass window?" Miles asked.

"I think that's what she called it," Colton said with a shrug.

Amy's heart sank.

Miles closed his eyes and put his hand to his forehead. "That window is probably priceless. I'm sure it's as old as the house."

"This isn't good," Amy said, dread filling her. "Especially because it's Beverly Brady."

"I'm sorry," Colton said. "I didn't mean to do it."

"I know." Miles sighed. "But you guys have to be more careful."

The boys looked duly chastised.

"I need to talk to her," Miles told them. "We'll need to pay for the window. I'm going to expect the two of you to work off the money that it will take to replace it."

"Yes sir," Colton and Matt said in unison, though neither one looked excited about the prospect.

"I'll go with you," Amy told him. "It'll probably be best if the kids stay inside. No doubt she's livid. We can't trust that she'll speak kindly to them."

"I agree."

They walked down the back stairway and into the kitchen. Amy had left her coat on a chair, so she put it on and zipped it up.

Miles held the door open for her, and she walked out in front of him.

Anxiety and dismay wound through Amy's heart as they walked side by side toward Beverly's home. They had a good view of her house, and Amy saw the broken window.

Beverly must have seen them coming, because she opened the back door as they crossed over the property line and onto her driveway.

"I knew something like this would happen." Beverly's face was red, and her eyes bulged with anger. "Those hooligans hit the puck through my gorgeous window on purpose! I just know it. Do you know how much that glass was worth? It's stood the test of time for over a hundred and twenty years—and then your sons come along and destroy it without a care in the world."

"The boys feel horrible about what happened," Miles said. "It was an accident, and they are very sorry."

"Sorry doesn't fix my window." Tears were in Beverly's eyes—but whether they were tears of anger or sadness, Amy couldn't tell. "I will expect that glass to be replaced. Do you know what that will cost you?"

"I imagine it's going to be very expensive," Miles said with a sigh. "I will gladly pay whatever it costs, and the boys will be working off the cost for—"

"The rest of their childhoods," Beverly finished, her arms crossed and her foot tapping fast on the porch floor. "I warned you something like this would happen. First my window—and what next? I live in constant fear that those children will ruin something priceless—and it happened. How soon until it happens again? Two of those children aren't even living here yet. What about when they're here full-time? Moppet and I cannot live like this."

"We're very sorry," Amy said. "The children did not do this on purpose."

"I almost wish they had." Beverly lifted her chin. "Then I could call the police and have them sent away."

"That's uncalled for," Miles said. "The children were playing a game, and they made a mistake. I think they'll be more careful in the future."

"More careful?" Beverly snorted. "I doubt they even know what that means."

Amy looked at Miles, and she could see his own anger was escalating. Just last night, they had talked about going the extra mile to draw Beverly into their lives. But she doubted Miles remembered that conversation at the moment.

"We are all very sorry," Amy said, trying to keep her voice even as she reached out and took Miles's hand. She gave it a gentle squeeze, to remind him of their plan. "We'll talk to the children again about respecting your property, and we'll pay for the window as soon as you let us know how much it will cost to replace. The boys will work off the cost and do their best to avoid repeating the mistake in the future. That's the best we can do, Mrs. Brady."

"I wish it was enough," she said. "But I highly doubt it." She turned to go back into the house but said over her shoulder, "You'll be getting a bill very soon."

Amy was shaking from head to foot—not only because of the cost of the window, but also because of the encounter with Beverly. Accidents happened, no matter how hard people tried to prevent them. It would be impossible to promise Beverly that the kids wouldn't make more mistakes in the future, no matter how much they talked to them.

They walked back to the house and entered the warm kitchen. As soon as Amy's nerves began to settle, the weight of the situation hit her, and all at once, she felt overwhelmed. Tears sprang to her eyes, surprising her.

"What's wrong?" Miles asked. "Beverly?"

Amy shook her head and then nodded. "It's all of it. Beverly, the wedding, the move, the missing veil. Someone purposely trying to make our lives more difficult. I'm just so tired of it all, and I want to take a long, quiet nap somewhere. But there's so much to do. I feel like I'm never going to get a quiet, peaceful moment to myself, ever again."

Miles drew Amy into his arms and held her as she let the tears fall.

"I know this is a lot," he said. "How about I keep Matt overnight too? You can go home and get into bed and sleep in a little tomorrow before work. I'll make sure they get to school, so you won't have to worry about them. And after I finish putting the bunk beds together and the kids have eaten and gone to bed, we'll choose a movie and cuddle up with some popcorn. You need some breathing room, and I'm going to make sure you get it."

Amy wiped her eyes and smiled up at him. "Thank you."

"Of course. I love you, Amy."

"I love you too."

He gave her a kiss and then said, "Let's go tackle the bunk beds and try to forget about the rest of it. I'd lecture the boys again, but I know they realize the severity of what they've done. It doesn't pay to make them suffer longer."

Amy nodded. She couldn't agree more.

The boys would be working off the cost of the window for years, and they weren't going to forget about it anytime soon.

Snow began to fall again, dropping from the dark sky like little lace doilies. There was no wind, and the flakes fell silently to the ground.

Inside the house it was a different story. Matt and Jana were in the upstairs bathroom fighting over who got the red toothbrush, while Natalie and Colton were in Colton's room fighting over a blanket. Natalie claimed it was hers, given to her by their grammy Anderson for Christmas, but Colton said she gave it to him. Colton had taken it out of Natalie's bedroom, and she had found it on his bed. He held one end of it while Natalie held the other.

Around and around they went about the blanket, while Matt and Jana fought about the toothbrush. Amy stood in the hallway, between the two fighting sets of siblings, her head aching from all the noise.

"Enough!" she said in a voice she reserved for very special occasions when she needed to get their attention. It was the same voice she used in her classroom when absolutely necessary.

All four children stopped fighting. Amy had a view of Matt and Jana but couldn't see Natalie and Colton from where she stood.

Matt's and Jana's eyes were wide. They were just as unused to hearing Amy raise her voice as Natalie and Colton.

"I'm tired of all the bickering," Amy said in a quieter, calmer voice. "And it's giving me a headache."

"I'm sorry, Mama," Jana said. She let go of the toothbrush, and Matt set it on the bathroom counter.

Miles came up the back steps from the kitchen, where he had been talking to his insurance provider to see if they would help pay for Beverly's broken window.

"What's going on?" he asked. He had probably heard her in the kitchen too.

Amy took a deep breath. "The kids are bickering, and I just need them to stop fighting and get ready for bed."

"Do you all hear that?" Miles asked.

"Colton stole my blanket off my bed," Natalie said.

"It's my blanket," Colton corrected. "Grammy gave it to me for Christmas."

"Nuh-uh," Natalie said in a whiny voice. "I got the blue one, and you got the green one."

"I don't know where the green one is," Colton said.

"That's not Natalie's problem," Miles told his son. He started to walk toward Colton's bedroom but then stopped and turned to Amy. "I'll deal with this one."

Amy nodded, relieved. "And I'll settle the toothbrush issue."

Fifteen minutes later, after Amy and Miles had tucked the kids into their beds and said their prayers with them, they walked down the steps and into the kitchen.

"Did you get an answer from the insurance company?" Amy asked.

Miles went to the cabinet and pulled out the air popper. "I had to leave a message. I hope to hear back from them in the morning."

Amy found a large bowl while Miles got out the popcorn kernels.

"I honestly don't know if I'll be able to stay awake long enough to watch a movie," Amy said with a yawn. "I'm exhausted."

"We don't have to watch a movie," Miles said. "I'd just like to spend a little time alone with you."

Amy smiled, despite her exhaustion. "I'll never turn down time with you. We can start a movie, but I don't know how late I'll stay."

"That's okay. I'll take you for as long as I can get you." He measured out the popcorn and put it into the machine then flipped the switch.

Amy's phone dinged with a text message.

"It's from Tracy," she said above the noise of the popcorn machine, quickly reading the text before telling Miles. A sinking feeling hit her stomach. "It looks like Tawny got back to her. She was able to locate Nora Tanner, and Nora said she thought Grandma Pearl came to the museum and picked up the veil after the exhibit closed."

Deep disappointment settled on Amy's shoulders. She pulled out a chair and took a seat, feeling like she might cry again. Where could it have gone? They had scoured the attic several times and couldn't find it anywhere.

Miles got out a pan to melt the butter. "What does that mean?"

"It means that if the veil came back to my grandma and we can't find it in the attic, it's gone. We don't have any more leads."

"I'm sorry, Amy." Miles crouched down in front of her. "I know how much it means to you."

"I'm going to have to buy a different veil," she said, almost in disbelief. "I'll be the first bride in the family to get married without it in a hundred years. Each bride who has worn it has been so happy in her marriage."

Miles touched her cheek and said gently, "It doesn't mean we won't be happy, Amy."

"I know." She set her phone on the table. "I just wanted to be a part of something special. I've felt left out of the marriage club for so long, I was looking forward to one of the privileges my sister and cousin were given. To wear our great-grandmother's veil is an honor. One I won't get."

The tears started then, and Amy couldn't stop them.

"We can start a new tradition," Miles said, standing and pulling her to her feet so he could hug her. "One that Natalie and Jana can carry on, if they'd like."

Amy clung to Miles and tried to see the silver lining in this situation too.

But she couldn't. She couldn't think of a single good thing that could come from the missing veil.

"Besides, we can't give up now," Miles said. "There's still time to find it."

"But we're out of ideas."

"Maybe something will pop up. You'll see. Keep the faith. You never know what will happen."

Amy hoped he was right. She wanted to believe that it was possible.

"Why don't you choose a movie and get comfortable?" Miles asked her. "I'll finish up the popcorn and bring it in to you."

"Are you sure?"

He nodded and kissed her forehead. "You need to take a breather."

Amy wasn't going to debate with him, so she left the kitchen with Scrappy in her arms and went into the family room. She pulled a thick blanket out of the basket and took a seat on the end of a couch. It was also a recliner, so she pressed the button and let it bring her feet up. After arranging the blanket and settling Scrappy on her lap, she turned on the television with the remote control and flipped through her choices until she found a movie that looked interesting.

She wasn't even through the opening credits before her eyes started to drift closed.

Suddenly, she startled awake.

"Amy?" It was Miles.

"Yeah?"

The lights were off in the room, and the end credits rolled on the movie.

"What time is it?" Amy asked, sitting up.

"It's after ten. The movie just ended."

Amy blinked several times. "I slept through the whole thing?"

He smiled. "I didn't have the heart to wake you when I came in. You were out cold."

He was sitting next to her on the couch, the half-eaten bowl of popcorn on the end table beside him.

She chuckled. "Was the movie good?"

His smile turned into a grin. "I'm going to be honest. I only watched about the first fifteen minutes, and then I fell asleep too. The end credits woke me up."

She snuggled up next to him and sighed. "I wish I didn't have to leave."

"Me either. Just thirteen more days."

Amy smiled to herself. "Thirteen more days." She closed her eyes, loving the feel of his arms around her. "I suppose I should go. I have a busy day tomorrow."

"I'll walk you out."

They left the family room and put Scrappy out while Amy pulled on her winter coat. It was going to be cold outside, so she used her remote start to turn on her car and get it warm before braving the dark.

"Are you feeling any better?" Miles asked after she zipped up her coat.

"A little," she said. "Thank you for letting me crash on the couch."

"Any time. I'm happy you're feeling a little better. All of this will soon be over, and we'll be married."

Amy nodded. It was the same thing she had been saying to herself for days.

"I think I'll take some cookies over to Beverly tomorrow," she said. "As a peace offering. And it'll give me an excuse to ask her about Mercy and the wedding vendors."

"Sounds like a good idea. I hope she's not still storming mad."

"Me too. But I'll take the risk."

"Maybe leave the kids at home," Miles suggested. "Just in case."

"We'll have to work on her one person at a time. Eventually she might be willing to accept all of us, but if I can get her to accept me for now, that'll have to be enough."

Miles winked at her. "I don't know how she couldn't love you."

Amy wished she shared his confidence. Maybe she'd feel more like herself in the morning.

Chapter Ten

Amy did feel more like herself the next day after a good night's sleep. She was even energetic with her students, tackling the to-do lists she had in her classroom. By the time the school day ended, she was ready to head to Miles's house and start to unpack some of the boxes they had brought over. She would work on the girls' room first, since Miles had finished the bunk beds and the girls were eager to get settled.

But first, she was determined to bake Beverly those cookies.

"These are some of my favorite cookies," Amy said to Jana and Natalie as she stood in the kitchen. Miles was on the second floor with the boys, helping Matt rearrange the furniture in the guest room to better suit his needs. They had brought the desk from Matt's old room and were trying to make space for it.

"What kind of cookies are they?" Natalie asked.

"Cranberry, pecan, and oatmeal," Amy said, wiggling her eyebrows. "I got them as a Christmas gift from one of my students at my old school in Steeleville. I loved them so much the student's mom gave me the recipe. They make a great gift."

"Is that why you're making them for Mrs. Brady?" Jana asked.

"Yes." Amy helped the girls combine the ingredients and start the mixer.

Miles entered the kitchen from the back stairs. "How's everything going in here?"

"Great!" Natalie said. She had a dab of flour on her chin. "I got to crack the eggs."

"And I got to put in the sugar," Jana added.

"I know there are about a million other things we should be doing right now," Amy said, trying not to feel guilt or pressure. She had dozens of boxes waiting for her to sort and organize, not to mention the bathrooms that still needed to be packed and moved from her old house.

"Maybe," Miles said as he went to the junk drawer in the kitchen and started to move things around. "But life shouldn't be all about work. We need to take time to have fun too. Even when we're on a tight deadline." He found whatever he was searching for and closed the drawer. "We're almost done in Matt's room. He wants to know if you want to help him organize his dresser and closet, or if you're going to let him do it by himself."

Amy had a vision of what Matt's closet and dresser would look like if he was left on his own. "I'll come up and help him after I drop off the cookies with Beverly. It shouldn't be more than forty-five minutes. Tell him he can start with his socks and pajamas. That should be safe enough."

Miles winked at her. "I'll try to keep an eye on him, and if we have any questions, I'll let you know." He started to head back toward the stairs but paused. "Oh, I heard from my insurance agent. He told me what I had suspected. Our liability insurance won't pay for Beverly's window. It's on us."

Amy nodded, already anticipating the news. It would be a big expense, especially now, paying for the wedding and hoping to remodel the third floor for the boys. Maybe that would have to wait for a bit.

Thirty minutes later, Amy left the house with a small disposable container of cookies. They smelled delicious and were so yummy, she had warned the girls not to eat more than one, or they'd spoil their supper.

The air was cold, and the freshly fallen snow from the night before sparkled on the neighborhood lawns. There was a piece of cardboard taped on Beverly's broken window from the inside. The glass had not been completely shattered, but there was a significant hole, and many of the pieces of stained glass had come loose.

Amy sighed and prayed for wisdom as she approached Beverly's back door. She wanted to be neighborly and kind, but she knew enough about Beverly to brace herself for a barrage of insults. Especially after yesterday's accident.

After knocking on the door, Amy stood on the cold porch and waited. Moppet began to bark inside, drawing closer to the door with each yip.

Soon the door opened, and Beverly stood on the other side. Behind her was a beautiful kitchen, spotless and expensive. Everything looked top-of-the-line—appliances, light fixtures, and cabinetry. A small desk sat near the door with a pad of paper and several pens on it.

Amy barely had time to take everything in before Beverly said, "What do you want, Miss Allen?"

"Hello, Mrs. Brady." Amy tried to focus on Beverly, though something on the pad of paper caught her attention. It was a familiar name. *Trish Henning.* The baker at Cake Creations.

Why would Beverly have Trish's name and phone number?

"The girls and I made some of my favorite cookies," Amy said, using all her willpower to smile at Beverly. "They're cranberry, pecan, and oatmeal. We thought you might like some. And I wanted to offer our sincere apology again for the window."

Beverly looked down at the container in Amy's hand and lifted her nose, as if the sight of the offering made her sick to her stomach.

"You think you can make things better by bringing me cookies?"

"No." Amy's gaze shifted to the pad of paper again, trying to see what it said, but it was hard to focus when she was trying to address Beverly. "I thought it would be a neighborly thing to do. I don't expect anything to make the situation better. But I think that time and kindness will help."

"What is that supposed to mean? You think that given enough time I won't dislike you anymore?"

"That's what I'm hoping." Amy's gaze darted to the paper again, and she saw the word *Gather*—the venue where she and Miles had planned to hold their reception.

"Well, it won't work," Beverly said, not even reaching for the cookies. "I don't want your apology or your cookies. I want peace and quiet and to be left alone." She frowned and glanced over her shoulder to see what had captured Amy's attention.

Amy looked harder at the list and saw the names, phone numbers, and addresses of her wedding vendors—the ones that she had originally booked. The ones that had been canceled.

"What is that list?" Amy asked.

"Oh, this?" Beverly tore the top page off the pad and folded it. "It's a list of wedding vendors for my nephew's fiancée, Mercy. She asked me to help find—" Beverly paused and frowned, crossing her arms. "I don't have to tell you what this is. This is my house and my business." Moppet started to bark near Beverly's feet. Beverly picked up the little white dog and held her close. "I'd like you to leave, Miss Allen. You're making Moppet upset. You can take your cookies and your apology with you. And tell Dr. Anderson that I've had some preliminary estimates for the window, and he's going to be shocked at the cost. I plan to replace the window with an antique of similar age and appearance, and they aren't easy to come by."

Amy groaned inwardly. "We are expecting it to be expensive."

"Double or triple whatever you think it will cost, and then prepare yourself for even more." Beverly started to close the door, causing Amy to back up. "And don't bring me any more food. I have too many allergies to mention. Plus, I don't like unwanted gifts—or neighbors."

Sighing, Amy returned to the house.

When she entered the kitchen, she found all four of the kids—and Miles—eating cookies.

"Hey," she protested. "Those are for after supper!"

"But they're so good," Miles said. "The kids and I were thinking we should just have cookies and milk for supper tonight."

Four heads bobbed in unison.

"The chicken is already thawing for fettucine alfredo," Amy said, shooing them away from the cooling racks. "I'm going to put these somewhere safe."

The kids protested but left the kitchen.

Miles stayed behind. "How did things go with Beverly?"

"Horrible." Amy set the container on the table. "She wouldn't take the cookies and warned me that she's been getting quotes and that the window replacement is going to be much more expensive than we realize."

"I've already suspected that."

Amy frowned. "But the strangest thing is that she had the names and phone numbers of all our vendors on a notepad. When I asked her about it, she became defensive and said she was just helping Mercy."

"Do you think she was the one who called all the vendors and canceled?"

"I have a sneaking suspicion that she was. But how can I prove it?"

Miles thought for a second. "I wonder if anyone has the phone number of the person who canceled your bookings. Maybe there's a record of it. If we got the phone number, we could call it and see who answers."

"That's a great idea!" Amy smiled. "I'll call Trish, since she was the one who was the most sympathetic to our problem."

Amy pulled out her phone and found the baker's number. A few seconds later, Trish was on the other end.

"Hello?" she said.

"Hi Trish, this is Amy Allen."

"Hey, Amy."

Amy explained why she had called, and Trish was happy to help her. It took a little time for her to look through her phone to find the right number, but thankfully, she remembered what day the caller had canceled the order.

"Here it is," Trish said. "Do you have a pen and paper ready?"

"I do."

Trish gave Amy the phone number and said, "Good luck. I hope you figure out who did this."

Amy ended the call and then quickly dialed the number that Trish had given her. After six rings, voice mail picked up—but it was a generic recording and didn't help Amy at all.

"Well," she said as she ended the call and set her phone on the counter, "I guess I can keep trying to call the number, but I doubt she'll answer if she has caller ID and knows it's me. It was a good idea. I wish it had worked."

"We'll figure this out." Miles tried to reassure her as he wrapped her in a hug. "You'll see."

Amy accepted his hug but quickly realized what he was doing. "You're trying to steal another cookie from behind me, aren't you?"

Miles laughed. "Who, me?"

She gave him a look as he lifted his hand and, with a huge grin on his face, took a big bite of a cookie.

Later that evening, after supper, Amy and Miles were back in the kitchen, cleaning. The boys were doing homework in their rooms, and the girls were watching a movie in the family room with Scrappy.

Amy's phone rang, but her hands were in the soapy water. "Can you get that?"

"Sure." Miles wiped his hands on a towel and went to the table where Amy's phone sat. "It looks like your Realtor, Carol."

"Oh." Amy quickly pulled her hands out of the water and wiped them on a towel as Miles answered her phone.

"Hello," Miles said. After a second he continued, "Sure. Amy's right here. I'll put you on speaker."

"Hi, Carol," Amy said as she set the towel on the counter. "What can I do for you?"

"Hi, Amy. Sorry to be calling during the supper hour."

"It's okay. We're done eating."

"Good. I'm calling because I have a question from the buyer of your house. I know I should have asked you days ago, but she just made the offer now. I told her it might be too late, but there's no harm in asking."

Amy's curiosity was piqued, and she looked at Miles, who shrugged. "What does she want?"

"She's moving from Florida, and she's planning to fly here. She's not bringing a moving van, because she doesn't want all the hassle. She's selling everything before she comes, so she'll be without any furniture in the new house. She's wondering if you'd be willing to sell some of yours. She saw the pictures I sent her, and she loves your style. I told her that you were getting married and combining households, so you might not need all of it. She's wondering if you'd be willing to sell it to her."

Amy glanced at Miles again, excited for something good to happen. She questioned him with a raise of her eyebrows, and he nodded, as if he thought it was a good idea too. "I'd love to sell it to her. I've been wondering what I was going to do with all of it, and it was just one more thing on my to-do list."

"Wonderful! I'll need a list of the items you'd like to sell and your asking price."

"I can get that to you right away."

"Perfect. Stephanie will be so pleased."

"Stephanie?" Amy asked.

"Oh, the buyer. Her name is Stephanie Fairbanks. She used to live in St. Louis but moved to Florida a few years ago. She misses Missouri and decided to move back here. She's excited to live in Canton."

"I'm happy it's working out for her." Amy couldn't contain her grin. "I'll email the list to you tomorrow. Will that be okay?"

"Absolutely. Thanks, Amy. Have a good night."

"You too. Bye." Amy pressed the red icon on her phone and looked up at Miles.

He wasn't smiling like she expected. Instead, he seemed a little upset.

"What?" Amy asked, her happiness slipping. "What's wrong? Don't you want me to sell my furniture?"

"No—I mean, yes. That's not what's bothering me."

"Then what is?" Amy tilted her head as she studied him.

"Nothing." He shook his head and went over to the sink. "It's—it's nothing. Really."

Amy frowned. "Something made you upset. Was it something Carol said?"

"It's nothing, Amy. I was just worried about something, but it's not a big deal." He smiled. "I'm happy that the furniture situation resolved itself. See, I told you things would work out."

Amy wasn't convinced by Miles's smile that he was okay, but if he wasn't willing to talk about what had made him upset, she wasn't going to force him. If it really was something serious, he'd tell her. Though she couldn't imagine what it would be. Getting rid of her furniture this way was the best thing that could have happened. Now she wouldn't have to worry about getting it sold or donated before the closing date.

All she needed to do was figure out what to ask for it. The extra money would help pay for the broken window at Beverly's house. But how much should she ask for? Too much, and the buyer wouldn't be interested. Too little, and she and Miles would miss an opportunity to help with their finances.

"As soon as we're done here," Amy said, "will you help me come up with a list and help me figure out how much to ask for the furniture?"

"Sure." But Miles seemed distracted as he finished washing the dishes.

And Amy was too excited about the furniture to dig deeper and find out what was bothering him.

When he was ready, he'd tell her.

Chapter Eleven

*D*on't worry about us," Tracy said as she stood next to Amy in her kitchen. "We'll get the bathrooms packed, and then I'll have the kids help me do a deep cleaning in the rest of the house."

"But I feel bad leaving," Amy protested. "You don't have to pack and clean while I'm gone."

"Go," Robin said, handing Amy her purse. "Enjoy a meal with your fiancé."

It was Tuesday, and Amy was meeting Miles at Les Trois Colombes to try out dishes for the wedding reception. Amy was certain they'd have the French restaurant cater for them, but she didn't know what she would select.

"You'll be late if you don't hurry," Tracy said, gently nudging Amy toward the back door. "Miles will wonder where you are."

"And you're sure you don't mind?" Amy asked her sister and cousin.

"No!" they both replied.

"Okay." Amy sighed. It wasn't easy asking for help. "Bye, kids."

Several voices called to her from different rooms in the house.

"Bye," Amy said to Tracy and Robin. "I'll be back as soon as I can."

"Take your time," Tracy insisted. "Seriously."

Amy smiled and stepped outside into the cold. The snow crunched under her feet as she walked to the garage. She would miss this house and all the good memories she had made there with the kids, but she was ready to move on.

A few minutes later, she pulled into the restaurant parking lot but didn't see Miles's Jeep. He was working late at the clinic today, a rare occurrence, because he had a meeting for the Blessings Convenient Care Children's Foundation. He was the chairman of the board of directors.

Amy walked into the restaurant and was immediately impressed. The atmosphere was warm and inviting, with a little whimsical charm. Grapevines hung around the ceiling, and gentle French music played over the speakers.

"Bonjour," the hostess said to her. "How may I help you?"

"I'm here for a wedding tasting."

"Amy Allen and Miles Anderson?" she asked.

Amy nodded.

The hostess smiled. "Please come with me. We have a table ready for you."

The dining room was just as beautiful as the lobby. It was quiet at this time of day, and there was only one other occupied table.

Amy was shown to her table, and a waiter came out with water and a baguette on a bread board.

"We have several dishes prepared for you," he said. "Would you like to start now, or wait for your fiancé to arrive?"

"I'd like to wait. Thank you."

"Let me know if you need anything else while you're waiting."

With a nod, the waiter left Amy alone at the table.

She glanced at her phone and saw that she was a few minutes late—which meant that Miles was also late. She didn't have any calls or texts from him, but she assumed his meeting went longer than expected.

Amy nibbled on the bread, her stomach growling. She hadn't eaten much that day, knowing she'd be filling up on French cuisine. It was four o'clock, a little too early for supper, but the restaurant had requested this time so Amy and Miles could have the undivided attention of the chef and the waiter.

Several minutes passed, and still, no Miles. He was rarely late, and, if he was, he always tried to call or text to let her know.

She was just about to call him when he walked into the restaurant, looking a little harried.

He saw her sitting in the dining room and said something to the hostess, then he walked to their table.

"Sorry I'm late." He gave her a quick kiss on the cheek and took a seat next to her. "The meeting ran over."

"That's okay," she said. "I suspected as much."

"The whole day has been one fiasco after another." He let out a breath. "But I'm here now."

"Good." She smiled. "Tracy and Robin are at the house with the kids, overseeing the last of the packing and cleaning. They told us to take our time and enjoy ourselves."

Miles returned her smile, but Amy could see that it didn't quite reach his eyes. There was something bothering him. Was it the hectic day at work, or something else?

The waiter brought out the first course. It was *salade de chèvre chaud*, a delicious goat cheese salad with green leaves, cherry tomatoes, walnuts, apples, olive oil, and balsamic vinegar.

After taking a few bites, Amy said, "I emailed the furniture list to Carol today. She sent it on to the buyer, and the buyer accepted our price."

"Yeah?" Miles seemed distracted as he took a bite of his salad. "That's good."

"Very good. What she's giving us for the furniture will help pay for Beverly's window."

"Great." Miles nodded.

Amy was about to ask him what was bothering him when the waiter approached to inquire what they thought of the salad.

"It's delicious," Amy said.

"Um, yeah, it's good," Miles added after a long pause.

"Wonderful. Next up, we'll have coq au vin, a traditional chicken dish cooked with wine, mushrooms, and bacon."

"Mm," Amy said. "My mouth is watering."

The waiter left again, and Miles focused on his salad.

"What's going on, Miles?" Amy asked.

He looked up at her. "I'm sorry. I'm just distracted."

"I can see that."

"It's nothing."

"You said the same thing last night."

"Because it's true." He smiled, and this time it seemed genuine. "I'll try my hardest to put work and everything else aside for the evening."

Amy smiled. "It's not easy, is it?"

Miles shook his head.

After the coq au vin, they enjoyed boeuf bourguignon, a thick beef stew with vegetables, and *hachis Parmentier*, a French version of shepherd's pie. All three were delicious, which meant Amy and Miles had a difficult decision to make.

"We know you are having cake at your reception," the waiter said as he cleared away their last dish. "But we want to treat you to three of our finest desserts." He smiled as another waiter appeared with a tray.

"We have beignets, chocolate-filled crepes, and crème brûlée. Bon appétit."

"Thank you," Amy said. "This is so generous."

"Thank you," echoed Miles. "I don't know how I'll possibly eat them all, but I'll give it the old college try."

The waiter laughed and left them with their dessert.

"Wow," Amy said as she looked down at her plate. "This food is amazing. Much better than the original caterer we'd selected."

"Another silver lining?" Miles asked with a wink.

"Yes." Amy grinned. "But now we have to decide which dish to serve. They were all so good."

"Which was your favorite?" Miles asked her.

"The boeuf bourguignon."

"Mine too."

"Then I guess it's not such a hard decision after all." Amy laughed.

Miles smiled at her. "Thank you for making me smile, Amy. It's been a challenging day, but you helped me forget about it. I'm so thankful that you're part of my life."

"I'm thankful for you too." All the angst Amy had earlier about Miles being distracted had eased, and she felt a lot better.

They told the waiter which dish they would like for their wedding and signed a contract. The restaurant would provide the salad, main dish, and baguettes for all their guests and a separate, gluten-free option for those who requested it. The meal would be unique and memorable. Exactly what they wanted.

"One more item off our to-do list," Amy said as they stepped outside the restaurant. "Now, back to the house, and we can finish up there. Only three more days before we turn it over to the new owner."

Miles offered Amy a tight smile and a brief nod, and that same distracted look returned to his eyes.

It was strange to walk through the empty house. Granted, some of the furniture was still there, like the dining room table, the living room couch, and the beds. But all the wall hangings were gone, the family pictures, the antiques, and the drawings the kids had made for Amy, which she had hung on her refrigerator.

Amy stood for a long time between the kitchen and the living room and just looked at the quiet space. Jana and Matt were already upstairs in bed. Miles had taken Natalie and Colton home with him over an hour ago, along with the last of the boxes. All that was left was the bedding and the items in their suitcases.

Everything else was gone.

The wind howled outside, but here, inside, Amy felt safe—if a little strange—in this house that had become a home for her, Matt, and Jana. They had only lived there for a couple of years, but it was enough to be woven into the fabric of her life story. The memories she had formed here were bright and colorful pieces of an ongoing tale. As soon as she sold the house on Friday, this chapter would end and another would begin. It was a poignant, bittersweet thought.

She had never been more ready for a change, and she had been through many of them.

Amy turned off the kitchen lights and walked through the living room into the entryway. Her piano had already been moved to Miles's house, so this space looked especially bare.

Three more nights in this house and then off to Tracy's for a week before the wedding. Amy felt like she was in limbo—but a good limbo. She would probably spend most of her time at Miles's anyway, unpacking the boxes they had moved to his house. It was kind of nice that they had been forced to do this quickly—a bit like ripping off a Band-Aid. It had been a lot of work, but now they wouldn't need to worry about moving things after the wedding. It also gave Amy time to spend at Miles's house in the coming week as a way to slowly ease into their daily routine. She and the kids would go to Tracy's to sleep, but that was probably all they'd do there.

Amy made sure the front door was locked then turned off the lights and climbed the stairs to the second floor where she could hear one of the kids already snoring softly.

A smile tilted Amy's mouth. She was thankful that Matt and Jana would have a dad and that Colton and Natalie would have a mom—and that the kids would have multiple siblings.

After checking on both the kids, who were fast asleep, Amy went into her own room. All that was left was her bed, her nightstand, and her suitcase.

She pulled back the covers and slipped into bed. She picked up her phone from the nightstand to see if she needed to charge it.

When she did, she saw that there was a text. It had come in twenty minutes ago, but she didn't recognize the number.

Frowning, she tapped the text icon.

MILES ANDERSON ISN'T WHAT HE SEEMS TO BE. HE'S HIDING SOME-THING FROM YOU—OR, SHOULD I SAY, SOMEONE. I'M DOING YOU A FAVOR. IF I WERE YOU, I'D STOP THIS WEDDING RIGHT NOW. IT'LL SAVE YOU, AND EVERYONE ELSE, A LOT OF HEARTACHE IN THE LONG RUN.

Amy stared at the text for a long time, her stomach turning as her palms began to sweat. Who would send her something like this? It couldn't possibly be true. Miles would never hide someone from her. The text insinuated that it was another woman. She couldn't believe him capable of something like that.

It was after eleven, but Amy couldn't sleep if she didn't speak to Miles about this. She would prefer to see him face-to-face and look into his eyes, but this couldn't wait until tomorrow. There was no way she'd get through a school day with this hanging over her head.

She called Miles, and the phone began to ring. Would he even be awake? He'd probably be worried to see her number at this time of night, but that didn't matter to Amy. This had to be addressed.

Her hands shook and her heart pumped hard as she waited for him to answer.

Finally, Miles answered. "Amy? Is everything okay?"

"No." Her voice shook too, and she felt sick to her stomach.

"What's wrong?" His voice held deep concern, and she could imagine what his face looked like right now. His eyebrows would be bunched together, and his brown eyes would be filled with worry.

"I just received a horrible text."

"Is someone sick or hurt?" he asked.

"No." She took a deep breath to try and steady herself. "I don't know who sent it, but they said you're hiding someone from me.

And that you aren't what you seem to be. It says I should call off the wedding."

"What?" Miles sounded just as shocked by the text as Amy was. "Who would do something like that?"

"I don't know." She swallowed hard. "Is this true, Miles?"

"Of course it's not true, Amy. I would never cheat on you, and I hope you know that. I don't know why someone sent that message to you, but there's absolutely no truth to it, whatsoever. I love you and only you, and I'm committing my life to you next week. I take that very seriously."

She was quiet for a moment, wanting to believe him and knowing that he had never done anything that would show her differently.

"I'm coming over, Amy," Miles said.

"No." She shook her head. "You can't leave the kids." Her heart rate started to settle. "All I needed was to hear your voice. I've never once suspected you of cheating on me, and I can't take this anonymous text seriously." She paused and then said, "Maybe this is another attempt to sabotage our wedding."

"Do you think that whoever canceled our vendors is the same person who sent you this text?"

"The numbers are different, but that doesn't mean anything. They could have used a friend's phone to text me."

"Whoever is doing this is not a good person. Why would they want to destroy our wedding?"

"I don't know, but I'm not going to let them steal our peace or excitement. I love you, Miles, and I trust you with all my heart. I know you would never hurt me this way."

"Of course I wouldn't. I love you too."

Amy took another breath. "Goodnight, Miles."

"Are you going to be okay?" he asked, his voice filled with a mixture of emotions. Concern, longing, uncertainty, and pain.

"Yes. I'm not going to let this bother me. Whoever sent that text is trying to sabotage our wedding for some reason, and I won't let them."

"I'm so sorry this happened."

"Me too."

"Goodnight, Amy."

"Goodnight. I'll see you tomorrow."

"See you tomorrow."

Amy ended the call and set her phone on the nightstand. She thought about erasing the text and blocking the number but decided to save it in case they needed it for evidence later. Whoever was doing this was being vindictive and hurtful. It had to be someone who would gain something if she and Miles didn't get married.

A thought struck Amy. Was this an attempt by Beverly to stop the wedding? Had she been the one to cancel all of Amy's vendors, and when that didn't work, had somehow gotten Amy's number and sent her a text with insinuations about Miles? After some of the things Beverly had said to Amy's face, she wouldn't put it past her to do something so conniving and manipulative.

All they needed to do now was prove it.

And put it all behind them.

Amy was marrying Miles in a week and a half, and she wouldn't let anything—or anyone—come between them.

Chapter Twelve

It was finally Friday, and Amy had taken the day off to sign papers for the house. There were a few large items that the buyer hadn't wanted or that Amy hadn't wanted to sell, like her antique steamer trunk and the shelves in the kids' bedrooms. Miles had also taken the day off, and Jeff had come by to help load everything into Miles's truck.

Amy stood in her kitchen after Miles and Jeff hauled out her antique rocking chair. It was the last thing to leave the house. The rooms looked so much bigger, and the noise bounced off the empty walls with an echo that reverberated in Amy's chest. It was bittersweet to say goodbye.

"Jeff had to get to work," Miles said as he came into the kitchen through the back door. "He said that if we need help this afternoon unloading the truck, he can stop by."

Amy took a deep breath. The past few days had been filled with wedding plans, unpacking at Miles's house, and an uneasy feeling about the text she had received. She and Miles had talked about it, but neither one knew who could have sent it. Amy didn't doubt Miles's faithfulness to her, but it still made her feel funny. Someone was clearly upset about their wedding and was trying to put a stop to it. She just wished she knew who it was.

"How are you doing?" Miles asked as he joined her at the counter.

"I'm okay. Sad, but also really excited to be moving on."

"And what about Matt and Jana? How are they feeling?"

"They were sad this morning when they left the house for the last time. I'm happy that they'll have school to distract them today."

Miles looked at his watch. "We should probably head over to the title company. Our appointment is in twenty minutes."

Amy nodded. "I'm ready."

Miles smiled. "So am I." He kissed Amy and gave her a hug before she grabbed her coat and purse and turned off the light in the kitchen for the last time.

She looked at the room for a second and then stepped through the door that Miles held open. After he closed it behind her, she locked it and put the key in her pocket.

It was a strange feeling to know she'd never enter the house again as the owner.

They walked to their vehicles, which were both loaded with the last-minute items they had taken out of the house.

Amy followed Miles to the title company and parked next to the building. He didn't need to be there, but she had asked him to come with her. It was nice to have someone by her side as she made big choices and life decisions. Another person to lean on and bounce ideas and problems off of.

"The new owner won't be here?" Miles asked as they walked into the building.

"No. Her appointment is later today," Amy said. "I'm not sure when, but they generally don't schedule these things on top of each other. I'll sign the papers on my end and give them the keys. Then the new owner will come in and sign her papers."

"Good." Miles nodded, appearing relieved.

Amy frowned, wondering why it mattered to him, though she didn't have long to think about it. Within twenty minutes all the paperwork was signed, Amy's questions were answered, and it was time to leave.

As they walked out of the conference room, the front door opened and an attractive woman walked in. Her thick blond hair was styled in waves over her shoulders, and her clothing looked expensive. She was tall, with a confident set to her shoulders.

She paused and pulled off her large sunglasses. Bright blue eyes were filled with surprise.

"Miles Anderson!"

Miles stiffened at Amy's side, and when she glanced at him, she saw apprehension in his gaze.

"Hi, Stephanie."

This had to be Stephanie Fairbanks, the new owner of her house. Why hadn't Miles mentioned that they knew each other?

"Imagine meeting you here," Stephanie said with a radiant smile. "I had heard you were back in Canton, but I didn't think I'd see you until I started work on Monday."

Miles glanced at Amy, an uncomfortable smile on his face.

"Do you know each other?" Amy asked him, though it was clear that they did.

"Yes." The smile seemed frozen on Miles's face.

"Know each other?" Stephanie's laugh sounded effortless. "We were practically engaged, weren't we, Miles? He asked me to marry him, but I was too concerned with my career at the time and told him no." She shook her head as she looked him up and down, regret on her face. "It was the biggest mistake of my life."

Miles had asked Stephanie to marry him? Amy's heart constricted, and her throat tightened. Why hadn't he told her? Especially when he learned that his old girlfriend was buying her house?

"I didn't ask you to marry me," Miles corrected, clearly uneasy as he shifted from one foot to the other.

"Not officially, I suppose," Stephanie said. "But we talked about it."

Amy felt like she was drifting on a life raft in the middle of the ocean with no land in sight. Was that why Miles had been acting so strange since Carol had told them the name of the new owner? But why hadn't he told her? Was he trying to hide something?

The anonymous text popped into her mind. Was Stephanie the person Miles was hiding from Amy?

Amy felt like she was going to be sick.

Stephanie looked at Amy. "I'm so sorry, how rude of me." She extended her perfectly manicured hand. "I'm Stephanie Fairbanks, Miles's old girlfriend."

Amy shook her hand, speechless.

"Oh," Miles said quickly. "Sorry. Stephanie, this is my fiancée, Amy Allen. Amy, this is Stephanie. We worked briefly together in St. Louis."

"I'm a traveling nurse," Stephanie said as she squeezed Amy's hand tighter than necessary. "At least, I was. I completed my nurse practitioner license and accepted a full-time position here in Canton at the Blessings Convenient Care Clinic. It'll be the first time I will own a house and the first time I'll put down some roots." She lifted her eyebrows. "What are you two doing here?"

Miles looked at Amy, who was still trying to process all the information. Not the least of which was that Stephanie had mentioned being a new hire at Miles's clinic. Both Miles and Stephanie were watching her. She had to say something. "I just signed papers to sell my house. I believe you're the buyer."

"I'm buying your house?" Stephanie asked, seeming more surprised than ever. "What are the odds of that?"

Amy's lips parted as she looked at Miles. What *were* the odds of that?

"Well," Miles said, putting his hand under Amy's elbow, "we should probably let you get to your appointment—"

"It just occurred to me that Carol said the seller was getting married and combining households." Stephanie looked between Miles and Amy. "You haven't gotten married yet, have you?"

Miles shook his head. "Next week."

Stephanie lifted one eyebrow. "So then, I'm not too late to put a stop to it?"

No one said anything for a second, and then Stephanie began to laugh. "I'm only teasing. I wish you both all the happiness in the world."

Amy looked at Miles, but he appeared unsure of what to say or do next.

"We have a lot to do today," Amy said. "It was nice meeting you, Stephanie."

"And you too," she said with her blazing smile. She put her hand on Miles's arm. "I'll see you on Monday. I'm looking forward to working with you again."

Amy blindly allowed Miles to lead her out of the building and into the cool morning air.

Neither one said anything as they walked to their vehicles. Amy didn't know what to say. She felt like she'd been blindsided by Stephanie—and Miles. Why hadn't he told her who Stephanie was?

"Amy," Miles said when they got to her car.

She finally looked at him, unsure if she should be hurt or angry because all she felt at the moment was confusion. "Why didn't you tell me you knew Stephanie Fairbanks?"

He took a deep breath. "Because I was hoping it wasn't the same Stephanie Fairbanks from my past. And because she didn't—and doesn't—mean anything to me."

"You've never even told me about her. If you were practically engaged, I think it's something I should have known."

"We were never even close to being engaged." He shook his head adamantly. "We had one conversation, once, about marriage, and it was more hypothetical than anything. She was a traveling nurse, and I asked her if she ever wanted to settle down and get married or have a family. It was a simple question and had nothing to do with me. I wasn't asking for myself. We worked together and went on a couple of dates. That's all. I knew, very quickly, that she wasn't someone I wanted to pursue. She wasn't right for me or for my kids. But we did see a lot of each other because we worked together. Nothing was ever inappropriate or serious. And when she told me she was moving on, I was relieved."

"Why didn't you ever mention her?"

"Because it wasn't serious. I honestly haven't thought about her in years—not until I heard her name the other day."

"And now she's going to be working with you." That was the part that bothered Amy the most. Miles was a good, upstanding man, but she didn't know Stephanie and didn't trust her, especially since she'd tried to mislead Amy into thinking there was more between herself and Miles.

"This is the first I've heard about her working at Blessings. And frankly, I'm not crazy about the idea. But I work with a lot of people. Some I get along with, and some I don't. You have nothing to worry about, Amy."

She took a deep breath. "I believe you."

"Stephanie likes attention," Miles said. "She said what she said to try to upset you. She used to do things like that all the time. Those were two of the many reasons I decided not to continue dating her and why I'm not looking forward to having her at Blessings. She can be difficult, even on the best of days."

"I understand. But Miles, once you heard her name, you should have told me who she was. You hid the truth, and that can be just as bad as lying."

"I know, and I'm sorry. I was hoping it wouldn't be the Stephanie Fairbanks I knew. I didn't even know she was living in Florida. When she left St. Louis, I had heard she'd moved to Maine or Michigan or somewhere. But that doesn't excuse my omission." He took Amy's hand. "But it was never serious, and it's not something you need to worry about."

Amy studied Miles's face and saw the deep sincerity there. She'd had a few boyfriends over the years that she had never mentioned to him because they were so insignificant. It was probably the same for Miles.

"Let's put this behind us," she said. "I wish you'd told me about her, but I understand why you didn't. You can't control where Stephanie lives or takes a job, so I know it's not your fault."

"Thank you." He looked relieved as he drew her into a hug. "I love you, Amy."

"I love you too."

When he pulled back, he said, "Let's take this stuff home and spend a few hours organizing before it's time to pick up the kids."

Amy smiled. She liked the sound of home.

"She's Miles's ex-girlfriend?" Tracy asked several hours later as she helped Amy unpack Jana's things in the girls' bedroom.

"'Ex-girlfriend' is a stretch," Amy said. "They went on a couple of dates, but Miles wasn't interested."

"But she said he proposed?"

"According to Miles, he asked her if she ever planned to give up travel nursing and settle down. She took that as a proposal of sorts, even though she admitted that he hadn't actually proposed. She said they talked about it."

Tracy lifted an eyebrow as she hung Jana's dresses up in the spacious closet. "Does she feel like a threat to you?"

"I'd be lying if I said it didn't bother me that they'll be working together. But I know Miles loves me. And I know that he works with a lot of attractive women. I don't doubt his faithfulness. What I struggle with is trusting her."

"From the little you've told me, she seems like the type to cause trouble on purpose."

"She acted surprised that she was buying his fiancée's house, but I wonder if she made the connection before today."

"There's no way of knowing." Tracy shrugged. "Was she surprised that Miles was engaged?"

Amy thought about it. She'd been so surprised that she hadn't been paying close attention to everything that had been said. She shook her head. "Not that I remember."

"So maybe she knew about you."

"She said she heard Miles was back in Canton," Amy said. "That much I know for certain."

"Hopefully she doesn't mean to cause any trouble," Tracy said as she hung up another dress.

"That's what I'm hoping too."

"You and Miles have so much to look forward to. Don't let someone like Stephanie ruin your happiness."

Amy nodded, trying to push aside her misgivings and apprehension. "I'll try not to."

"Good." Tracy pulled a dress from the box and held it up, ready to move on to a different topic. "Hasn't Jana outgrown this one?"

"Yes, but it's one of her favorites. She won't let me get rid of it."

Tracy chuckled. "I remember those days with Sara. It feels like so long ago."

Amy tried to focus on the dress, but she needed Tracy's opinion. "Do you think Stephanie Fairbanks is the person who tried to sabotage our wedding?"

"Why would you think that?"

"It was something she said. When she found out that Miles and I weren't married yet, she said something along the lines of, 'Good. I'm not too late to stop it.'"

Tracy frowned.

"She tried to laugh off her comment," Amy continued, "but it didn't sit right with me. Nothing about her sits right with me. I thought it might be jealousy at first, but—"

"It's okay to trust your gut, Amy. She has a motive for stopping the wedding—at least, it appears that she does. She said walking away from Miles was the biggest mistake of her life, right?"

"Yes."

"Then, maybe she regrets not staying in St. Louis to pursue a relationship."

"He said he wouldn't have continued seeing her even if she had stayed."

"Maybe she doesn't know that, or maybe she wants to change his mind." Tracy shrugged. "That would indicate a motive."

"So you think it could be her?"

"It could definitely be her. Trish said the woman who called to cancel your cake order sounded like she was about your age."

"That's right."

"Maybe it was Stephanie. I wouldn't rule her out."

"But how will I find out?"

"I don't know. And she didn't succeed, so I wouldn't be too worried."

"She moved all the way here from Florida, perhaps with the intention of trying to steal Miles from me. That makes me very worried."

"You still have the number from Trish, right?"

"Yes."

"Call it again and see who answers."

Amy pulled her cell phone out of her back pocket and found the number in her call history. It rang several times, but then a generic voice mail answered. "Nothing."

"Can you look up the number online? See if it's a Florida number?"

"I can try." Amy googled the number. "It's a Missouri area code."

"So it's not a Florida number?"

"No."

"Well," Tracy said, "that doesn't necessarily rule her out." She paused. "Maybe she got the number while she was in Missouri and never changed it to a Florida number. What about the anonymous text you got the other day? The one that claimed Miles was hiding someone from you. That was a different number, right?"

"Yes." Amy opened her text app and found the number. She copied it and then pasted it into the search engine. "This one is a Florida number."

"I bet Stephanie is the one who texted you, which means she knew who you were before she even met you."

"I'm going to call this number." Amy's heart pounded hard as she pressed the call button.

The phone rang and rang, but no one picked up. A generic voice mail message answered, so Amy hung up, frustrated. "No one answered this one either."

"If it's Stephanie, she won't answer your call. What you need to do is call the number when you're near her and see if her phone rings."

"I don't ever want to be near her again."

"It might be the only way you'll know if she's the one who texted you. If she was, it's a good indication that she's trying to break up your relationship with Miles."

Amy pressed her lips together then said, "I suppose I could try to find a reason to stop over at the house, but I really don't want to see her again."

"You can always talk to Miles about it and see what he thinks you should do."

"He'll probably tell me to let it go."

"Maybe. Maybe not."

Miles and Jeff were hauling things into the house from the Jeep. It was two thirty, and they'd need to pick up the kids soon. Maybe she could talk to him before they left for the school.

"Let's go find the men," Tracy suggested after she hung up the last of Jana's dresses.

They both grabbed empty cardboard boxes and took them down the stairs and into the kitchen.

Miles and Jeff were carrying in Amy's antique steamer trunk.

"Where do you want this?" Miles asked.

"I was thinking it would be a good place to store blankets in the family room," Amy said.

She and Tracy followed the men so Amy could decide where to put it.

"I think it'll look great under this window," she said, pointing to the spot.

The men set it down, and Jeff winced as he stretched his back. "Moving is a young man's game."

Miles put his hand on Jeff's shoulder. "We sure do appreciate your help." He looked at Tracy. "We couldn't have done this without you."

"We know you would do the same for us," Tracy said. "Don't think twice about it."

"We plan to take you two and Terry and Robin out for a nice meal after the wedding," Amy said, "when things are a bit more settled."

"That's not necessary," Jeff said, "but I won't turn down an invitation that involves food."

Amy glanced at the wall clock and said, "We should probably head out to pick up the kids."

"And we should get home," Tracy said. "Jeff's waiting for a delivery."

Amy put Scrappy in his crate, and the two couples left the house. Tracy and Jeff pulled away, and as she and Miles got into the Jeep, Amy said, "We're going to need to think about getting me a bigger vehicle."

"We'll need to wait until after the wedding, when we have a little more time to go shopping."

Amy nodded, unsure how to broach the topic of Stephanie again, though it was foremost on her mind. She decided to just face it head-on. "I'm not a fan of bringing up Stephanie's name, but I've been wondering. Do you think she was the one who texted me that horrible message? Tracy and I looked up the number, and it's from Florida."

His eyebrows rose. "I hadn't even considered it, but it's possible. Stephanie wasn't the most popular person at the hospital where we worked. She didn't have a lot of friends, and many of the other nurses complained she was difficult to work with. It doesn't say a lot about a person's character when all their coworkers dislike them."

"I tried calling the number, but no one answered. Tracy thought that if I call it when I'm with Stephanie, I might be able to hear it, if it's hers."

"That would be one way to figure it out. But I really don't want to think about it anymore. Whether it was Stephanie or not, whoever did it was just trying to cause trouble. We don't need to worry."

It was the same thing Tracy had said, but Amy couldn't forget about it so easily. Whether it was the compounded stress of the wedding and the move, or whether it was simply her own insecurity about Miles working with Stephanie, she felt compelled to get to the bottom of it.

Someone was out to hurt her and Miles, and she wouldn't let it rest until she knew who it was and why they were doing it.

Chapter Thirteen

"We're all moved out?" Jana asked Amy when they arrived at Miles's house. "We can never go back to our house again?"

"Yes, we're all moved out," Amy said. "And no, we can't go back to our old house again. This is our only home from now on."

Jana looked out the window at Miles's large, Victorian house, but it was hard for Amy to read her daughter's thoughts. Was she excited, nervous, sad?

"Come on," Natalie said, taking Jana by the hand. "Let's go play in our castle."

Whatever Jana felt about the big move was quickly forgotten as she and Natalie jumped out of the car and raced toward the house.

Amy sat for a second after the others got out of the Jeep, just soaking up the moment. This was her home. Her and Miles's home. Her children's home. All of it was still so new and overwhelming, in a good way.

Miles knocked on Amy's window, a smile on his face.

She opened her door.

"Everything okay?" he asked.

"It's perfect." Amy stepped out of the car as Colton and Matt disappeared inside the house. "It'll just take some time to get used to."

"Just think," Miles said after Amy closed her door and they started to walk toward the house, hand in hand. "Next week at this time, it'll be the day before our wedding. And two weeks from today, we'll have been married almost a week." He squeezed her hand. "Thirty years ago, when I went off to college with a broken heart, I wish I'd known this day was coming."

Amy leaned into him. "I'm sorry I broke your heart."

"You don't need to apologize. God worked it all out."

"I'm still sorry," Amy said. "I was a silly kid who didn't know what a big mistake she was making. But I figured it out fast."

"It's a good thing God can redeem our mistakes. With Him, nothing is impossible."

They'd started up the back steps when the door flew open and Jana appeared, her eyes wide. "I forgot Piggy!"

Amy and Miles came to a halt.

"What?" Amy asked.

"Piggy! I left Piggy at our house."

Amy walked up the rest of the stairs and put her hand on Jana's shoulder. Her daughter was shaking. Piggy was the stuffed animal that Amy had given to Jana when she had come to live with her. "I packed Piggy a couple of days ago. He's here already."

Jana looked up at Amy, her eyes wide as unshed tears gathered. "I found him and snuck him back so I could sleep with him. I didn't want you to know because I thought you'd take him again."

Amy knelt beside her. "It's okay, Jana."

"I want Piggy!" Jana cried, and she threw herself into Amy's arms.

"Where did you leave him?" Miles asked.

"In the cubby in my room," Jana said.

Amy knew what cubby she was talking about. There was a door in Jana's second-floor bedroom that led to the unfinished part of the eaves and had been used for storage. Amy had glanced into the cubby before leaving the house, but if the piglet was in a dark corner, she wouldn't have seen it.

"Are you certain you left Piggy in the cubby?" Amy asked.

Jana nodded. "I put him there yesterday morning, before we went to school, and I forgot to take him out." Her tears started all over again. "I want Piggy!"

Miles put his hand on Jana's shoulder. "We'll get Piggy back, I promise. I know who bought the house. Your mom and I can stop over there and see if she'll get him for us."

"What if she doesn't?" Jana asked, staring up at Miles with big eyes.

"She will," he reassured her. "Don't worry about it, okay? We'll take care of this for you. I promise."

Jana sniffled and wiped away her tears.

Miles opened the door for her, and she ran into the kitchen.

Amy stayed on the back stoop. "It looks like we're going to have to face Stephanie again after all."

"I can ask her about it on Monday at work so you don't have to see her, if you'd like."

"No." Amy shook her head. "Jana will be miserable until we get Piggy back. She'll ask us about him a hundred times between now and Monday, and then we'd have to rely on Stephanie remembering to bring him to you. We might as well stop over there now and see if she'll get him for us."

"Are you sure?"

Amy nodded.

The boys were old enough to stay home alone and could watch the girls for the few minutes it would take to run over to the old house. Amy and Miles told the kids to stay inside and not use anything in the kitchen while they were gone, and then they jumped into Miles's Jeep and headed toward Stephanie's house.

"This feels strange," Amy said as Miles turned down the street. "I only owned it a few hours ago, but it somehow feels like years have passed."

Miles smiled. "It's strange how things change so quickly in our minds."

"And how some things stick around much longer than we'd like."

They pulled up in front of the house. An unfamiliar car was parked near the garage, but nothing else looked different.

"She'll probably be surprised to see us," Amy said as she unbuckled her seat belt.

"I'm sure she will be."

They walked up the sidewalk together, and Amy pushed the doorbell. It was odd that she couldn't go right in. She had to get permission.

The door opened, and Stephanie stood there, her blue eyes wide with surprise. "I didn't know I was going to see you two again so soon. Miss me?"

Amy glanced at Miles, who looked rigid and uncomfortable. It felt odd, since he was usually so relaxed and easygoing.

"My daughter forgot her stuffed pig in the storage cubby upstairs," Amy said. "She forgot to tell me it was there, and we left it by accident. We were hoping we could get it back."

"Oh, and here I was thinking you'd come because you wanted to get to know me better." Stephanie sighed dramatically, but Amy knew she was trying to be funny. "Come on in."

She opened the door wider for them and moved aside as they entered.

Not much had changed, though Amy could see into the living room from the entry, and Stephanie had already moved the furniture around.

Stephanie closed the door behind them. "Feel free to go upstairs and search for as long as you need to, Amy. I'll keep Miles company down here while we wait." She took a step closer to Miles and laid her hand on his arm. "We have so much catching up to do. Don't we, Miles?"

It didn't seem possible that Miles could look more uncomfortable, but he did.

"I'll help Amy," he said. He moved away from Stephanie and put his hand on Amy's lower back and guided her to the stairs. "We won't be long."

Stephanie's eyes squinted in displeasure for a heartbeat, but she soon recovered. "I'll join you. I haven't investigated the storage areas of the house yet."

Amy led the way upstairs with Miles and Stephanie following her. When they got into Jana's old bedroom, she switched on the light and then crossed to the cubby door.

"I'm excited to start working at Blessings," Stephanie said to Miles. "I'd love to know more about the people and the work environment before I get there on Monday. Could we meet for coffee to chat? Are you free tomorrow?"

Amy waited to hear what Miles would say.

"That's not going to work," he said. "We're much too busy with the move and the wedding preparations."

Amy opened the cubby door, turned on her cell phone light, and flashed it around the storage area. Piggy was tucked into the corner, just like Jana had said.

"I found him." Amy had to bend to get into the tight space, but she was able to grab the stuffed pig. Then she remembered the Florida phone number.

She pulled up the app, found the text, and pressed the call button.

A phone outside the cubby began to ring.

Amy stepped out of the storage space, her pulse racing as she met Stephanie's shocked expression.

Stephanie held her phone in her hand, and it was still ringing.

"It *was* you," Amy said. She pressed the red button to end the call.

"What was me?" Stephanie asked, slipping the now silent cell phone into her pocket.

"You texted me on Tuesday night, telling me that Miles was hiding something from me—or rather, *someone*."

For the first time since Amy met Stephanie, the woman looked uneasy. She swallowed hard. "What do you mean?"

"You know what I mean," Amy said. She pulled up the text and turned her phone around so Stephanie could see. "You tried to get me to believe that Miles was hiding something from me."

"Well," she said, flustered. "He is!"

"What are you talking about, Stephanie?" Miles asked. "I'm not hiding anything from Amy."

"You're hiding me." Stephanie lifted her chin. "Did she know about us, Miles?"

"What was there to know?" Miles asked, anger and confusion in his voice.

"That you and I were engaged—and that we were going to reconcile."

"What?" He shook his head, frowning. "We were never engaged, and there was no hope of reconciling, because there was nothing to reconcile. You purposely misled Amy."

Stephanie didn't speak, but her chin went higher.

"Were you the person who canceled all our wedding vendors too?" Amy asked, almost certain Stephanie was the culprit.

"What are you talking about?" Stephanie asked with a bewildered look on her face.

"Someone canceled all our vendors a couple weeks ago," Amy said. "If you sent me a text, trying to sabotage our relationship, then it's clear you could have done that too."

"I'm not even going to answer such a stupid question."

"That's enough," Miles said. "It's time for us to go."

He led Amy out of the room and down the steps.

Stephanie followed.

"I'll see you on Monday," she said to Miles as if nothing had happened.

"Don't come around me," Miles said over his shoulder. "I have nothing more to say to you."

"Well, that's a crummy welcome," Stephanie said under her breath.

They walked out of the house, and Miles closed the door behind them. "That's the last time we'll ever need to come here again," he said.

"I was wondering how I'd come to terms with leaving it," Amy said as they walked to his Jeep. "Now I have complete closure. I hate knowing she's the new owner, but it makes me want to never set foot in that house again."

"Same here."

They got into the Jeep, and Miles didn't waste a moment pulling away from the house.

"Piggy!" Jana cried when Amy handed her the stuffed animal. "You found him!" She wrapped her arms around Amy and then around Miles. "Thank you, thank you, thank you."

"You're welcome," Amy said. "Don't hide him in any more cubbies."

"I won't. I promise." Jana ran toward the stairs and disappeared, calling Natalie's name.

Amy and Miles stood in the front entryway, looking at one another.

"I'm sorry about all of that," Miles said.

"At least we know now that Stephanie sent the text. I just wish we knew if she was the one who orchestrated the rest of our trouble. Even if she didn't call the wedding vendors herself, she could have asked a friend to do it."

"I'm sure she had one or two here in Missouri, though I doubt there are more. I'm telling you, she wasn't well liked."

"Yet you went on a couple dates with her?" Amy tilted an eyebrow, half-teasing, half-serious. "Makes me wonder if I can trust your judgment, Dr. Anderson."

"Hey," he said with a twinkle in his eye, "I'm marrying you, aren't I? I have the best judgment in the world."

Amy smiled.

"Besides," he said, "I took Stephanie out when she first came to St. Louis, before I knew how everyone else felt about her. And I only went on two dates because it didn't take me long to realize she wasn't the girl for me. Poor judgment would have been continuing to date her even after I learned the truth."

Amy gave him a hug. "I suppose you're right."

He smiled down at her. "All's well that ends well."

"Is this ended?" she asked. "We still don't know who canceled our wedding vendors. They still have a week to try to attack again."

"Then we need to keep our eyes open and be on the lookout, because I don't want anything to hinder our wedding plans."

A buzzing sound came from Amy's purse. "Someone's calling me," she said, pulling away. When she looked at her phone, she said, "It's Tracy."

"I need to get supper started," Miles said. He winked and then left her to talk to Tracy.

"Hey," Amy said. "What's up?"

"I'm at Robin's store. I was wondering if you wanted to swing by and visit Celebrations Bridal to look for a veil."

Amy let out a disappointed breath. "I was hoping not to have to buy one."

"I know. I'm sorry, Amy. I wish we would have had better luck finding ours. Are you free to stop by?"

There was a lot of unpacking and organizing to do, but it could wait. She needed a veil, and there was no better time to find one. "I'll let Miles know, and I'll meet you at Celebrations in about fifteen minutes."

"Perfect. See you there."

A few minutes later, Amy pulled up to the bridal store in downtown Canton. She had found her wedding dress there and had also picked out the two bridesmaid dresses Tracy and Robin would wear and the flower girl gowns for Jana and Natalie. She'd been there often.

"Hello, Amy," the shop owner, Patrice, said when Amy walked in the front door. "Tracy is already over by the veils."

"Thank you," Amy said. She bypassed the front desk and joined her sister.

"Hey." Tracy held up a waist-length veil. "What do you think about this one? It kind of looks like our veil."

Amy shrugged. "If I can't wear the original, I want something completely different."

Tracy set the veil back on the rack.

After Amy tried on a dozen or so veils, she settled on a simple fingertip-length one without a headpiece. It had a comb, which would get tucked into her updo.

It was nothing like the family veil.

"Are you sure this is the one?" Tracy asked her.

Amy nodded. "I don't want anything fancy."

They took it to Patrice, and Amy made the purchase, but before they left the shop, Tracy stopped her and pulled something out of her purse.

"I know you and the kids will be over later, but I thought I'd give this to you now, while I'm thinking about it."

"What is it?"

Tracy laid a handkerchief on Amy's palm. "It's one of Great-grandma Vivian's handkerchiefs that she embroidered."

There was a bluebell embroidered into the delicate fabric and blue scalloped edging.

"It's beautiful," Amy said.

"I thought if you can't have Great-grandma Vivian's veil, then at least you could carry one of her handkerchiefs. It's something blue, after all, and old and borrowed. So it ticks off several items on the 'something old, something new, something borrowed, something blue' list."

Tears sprang to Amy's eyes, and she wrapped her sister in a tight hug. "Thank you."

"I'm sorry we couldn't find the veil for you," Tracy said. "I'll regret that for the rest of my life."

Amy pulled back and wiped her eyes. "It's no one's fault. We'll just need to move on without it."

Tracy shook her head. "I won't give up. It has to be somewhere. We still have time."

Amy let out a sigh. She didn't want to be more disappointed than she already was. She tucked away her hopes and dreams of finding the veil and determined to accept the new one instead.

Chapter Fourteen

*T*he weekend sped by in a flurry of unpacking and organizing. Amy ended up putting more things in the donation pile than she anticipated, since there were several items that Miles already owned. Some of Miles's things were also sent to the donation pile, if Amy's were in better condition or had more sentimental value. Matt and Jana wanted to sleep at their new home, so it was only Amy who had gone to Tracy's on Friday and Saturday night.

By Sunday afternoon, when Amy, Miles, and the kids arrived at Tracy's house after church, Amy was happy with the amount of work they had accomplished. She was tired but satisfied.

"What are we having for lunch, Aunt Tracy?" Matt asked when they entered the house.

"We decided on a taco bar today," Tracy said as she helped hang up the kids' coats in the entryway. The weather had taken a cold turn, and snow was forecasted for several days. Amy kept an eye on her weather app as the wedding approached, and right now, everything looked like it would pass by before Saturday.

"Yummy," Natalie said, grinning. "I love tacos."

"Everyone likes tacos, silly," Colton said.

"Not everyone," Tracy said, "but most people."

Amy had stopped by the grocery store before heading back to Tracy's to buy lettuce, tomatoes, and sour cream. She handed the bag of ingredients to Tracy as she slipped off her shoes.

"We'll have a packed house today," Tracy said after the kids ran off to play. "Sara and Kevin are here with Aiden and Zoe, and Robin and Terry will be here any second with Kai."

"Great." Amy loved when the house was full.

"Don't you have some things you need to get done for the wedding today?" Miles asked Amy.

"What do you need to get done?" Tracy asked.

"It's nothing," Amy said. "I'll take care of it later tonight."

"You're going to Miles's to unpack this evening, aren't you?" Tracy asked.

"I just need to get the place cards filled out. I can do it when I come back here before bed."

"You'll be worn out by then," Tracy said. "We can work on the place cards after lunch. They'll get done a lot faster that way."

"Tracy, I've already asked way too much from you."

"First of all, you didn't ask me to help with the place cards. I offered. And second, you need to stop being afraid to ask for help, Amy. I know you're capable of a lot, but you're not Wonder Woman. We all need assistance once in a while."

"That's what I keep telling her," Miles said as he hung up his coat. "Maybe you can convince her, Tracy."

"I've been trying for weeks," Tracy said with a sigh. "Nothing speaks louder than burnout, though."

Amy took a deep breath. "I'm trying to do better. I just hate asking busy people to do more. I know how hard it is when someone asks me to help them. I almost always have to rearrange my schedule or take time away from my own responsibilities. I don't want to be a burden to you guys."

"We've all been put here to help each other," Tracy reminded her. "Right now you need help. Another time it'll be me. It all evens out in the end."

"Your sister is right," Miles said to Amy. "I want you to enjoy yourself this week before the wedding. It's hard to do that when you're overwhelmed."

"Okay, okay." Amy laughed. "I can't say no to you two when you're ganging up on me. I'll bring the place cards downstairs later, after lunch, and everyone can help me fill them out."

"Good," Tracy said. "It won't take long if we all pitch in."

Amy wasn't sure why it was so hard to ask for help. Maybe because she had been single for a long time and was used to being independent, or maybe it was guilt about infringing on other people's time. Perhaps, though, the biggest reason was pride. She didn't want to admit that she wasn't Wonder Woman, as Tracy had said—and she didn't like to face her own inadequacies. It was something she knew that God wanted to work on with her. Pride wasn't an issue He took lightly.

The kitchen was crowded and loud as everyone gathered to make their tacos. Amy loved watching Miles, Colton, and Natalie interact with her family. They had slipped into place without any effort and seemed to enjoy these weekly meals as much as the rest of them. It was the perfect opportunity for Amy's family to tell embarrassing stories about her past, though, and all she could do was grin and bear it.

"We never told you about the time Amy was supposed to play an angel in the Christmas pageant at our church?" Robin asked Miles. They were sitting around the dining room table, their meal finished.

"No," Miles said. He looked at Amy. Even though they had dated in high school, there were still stories he hadn't heard.

"If you haven't heard it by now," Amy said, her cheeks warm at the memory, "then you probably don't need to hear it."

"I've been waiting my whole life to hear it," Miles said with a teasing chuckle. "I want to hear every story about you."

Amy rolled her eyes and said to Robin, "You might as well get it over with."

Robin grinned. She loved telling this story. "I was in first grade, and Amy was in fourth. I was so excited because it was the first year I could audition for the pageant. I looked up to Amy so much and thought she was the coolest kid I knew, and I wanted to be exactly like her."

Miles grinned at Amy, and she just shook her head, knowing what was coming.

"When it was time to audition, I heard that Amy wanted to play one of angels. Since there was a whole host of them, I wanted to audition as an angel too."

"In my defense," Amy protested, "I was told that the angels were going to be dressed up like rockstar backup singers that year and not like typical angels."

"To this day, we have no idea where she heard that," Tracy said with a laugh.

"You told me," Amy protested. "I still think you did it to trick me."

Tracy only laughed again and shook her head.

"So," Robin continued, "everyone said that a first grader wasn't going to get chosen for the part of an angel, but I auditioned anyway, and I got a part—and so did Amy. I was so excited. I thought I had hit the big time."

Amy smiled at her cousin, knowing the good—and most embarrassing—part was coming.

"It turned out that the angels were just regular angels," Robin said. "With white gowns and golden halos. Amy was so disappointed she cried and didn't want to put on the costume and go on stage."

"To continue my defense," Amy said, "my best friends were given the roles of children who were learning about the nativity story, and they could wear whatever they wanted. They went out and bought pretty dresses, and I was stuck with a horrible, discolored bedsheet that was at least thirty years old. I wanted to quit, but Mom wouldn't let me."

"Whatever her reason," Robin said, "Amy got really nervous before the show. She was the only angel that had lines, but she couldn't remember them before it was time to go on stage."

Amy buried her warm face in her hands, and Miles laughed and put his arm around her.

"She was so nervous," Robin said, "that she froze backstage and refused to go on. I was supposed to go on with her, though I didn't have any lines. When our cue came, Amy wouldn't budge, so I pushed her as hard as I could. You can imagine what happened next."

"I'll tell it," Amy said, finally accepting that this story would follow her to her grave. She sat up straight and lifted her chin. "Robin pushed me right onto the stage. My feet got tangled in my nasty gown, and I knocked over the Christmas tree, which fell toward the manger. Mary screamed and had to grab the Baby Jesus doll and jump out of the way, but when she did, she and Joseph hit the wall behind them. It came crashing down, and everyone who was standing behind it waiting to come on stage went running in all directions, and the rest of the set was destroyed. There was so much chaos and so many screaming children, the pastor ran onto the stage and yelled, 'Merry Christmas to all, and to all a good night,' ending the program before it had barely begun."

Miles stared at Amy, and she could tell he was trying hard not to laugh.

"Go ahead," she said. "You can laugh. It's a lot funnier now than it was then." Her lips twitched as she tried to repress her own smile.

"That was you?" Miles asked.

"What do you mean?"

"That story was legendary. I wasn't at the pageant, but it was all anyone could talk about at school. I heard the whole church burned down."

"That's not true!" Amy declared, which only made Robin and Tracy laugh harder.

"I know that now, but when I was a kid, I believed it." He shook his head. "I can't believe that was you."

The rest of the family roared with laughter.

"Yes, that was me." Amy couldn't help but laugh with them. As a child, she'd been mortified to see everyone laughing. Thankfully, she could take the teasing about it now. "It was the most memorable Christmas pageant in the history of our church."

"That's one way to look at it," Tracy said.

"I think it's adorable," Miles said, hugging Amy to his side. "I just hope you don't have a repeat performance at our wedding."

She playfully nudged him as he continued to laugh, though there was a small part of her that was worried about the same thing. Maybe not to the same degree, but with all the trouble they'd had in the past couple of weeks, she had a feeling that something would go wrong. She just hoped it would be something they could all laugh about one day.

Amy woke up on Monday morning feeling strange. As she lay in the guest bedroom at Tracy's house, she couldn't quite place what was bothering her. She'd set her cell phone alarm fifteen minutes earlier than she normally did. She had told Miles that she would stop by and pick up Colton and Natalie before she headed to school so he wouldn't have to worry about taking them.

But that wasn't what was making her feel strange.

She had been sleeping at Tracy's house since Friday night, so that wasn't it either.

Amy tossed aside the comforter, put her feet on the ground, and suddenly realized what was making her feel this way.

Today was Monday, and Miles would be going to work with Stephanie.

She tried to push aside the uneasiness she felt, since she trusted Miles completely. But as she dressed and then got the kids up to get them ready for school, she couldn't deny that her discomfort was more about Stephanie than it was about Miles. Stephanie had been the one to send that text. What else might she be capable of? Amy didn't want to find out.

Yet, there was little she could do about the arrangement. She would have to get used to the idea and trust that God had His hand in the situation.

The smell of coffee met Amy's nose as she came down the back stairs and into Tracy and Jeff's kitchen. "Mm," Amy said, "there's nothing better than a fresh cup of coffee in the morning—except when someone else makes it for you."

"Good morning," Tracy said with a smile. "Are the kids coming down soon? Jeff's making pancakes for them."

"Matt's combing his hair, and Jana is brushing her teeth. They should be ready in a couple of minutes."

A stack of pancakes sat on a plate next to Jeff as he poured another ladle of batter onto the skillet. It crackled and steamed. "I miss having kids to cook breakfast for," he said. "Tracy is usually good with something light to eat. I hate cooking a big meal just for myself."

"You can make as many big breakfasts as you want this week," Tracy said, pulling a few plates out of the cupboard. "I intend to spoil my niece and nephew as much as possible before they move into Miles's house full-time."

Amy grinned and poured herself a cup of coffee. "Thanks for letting us bunk here for the week."

"Our pleasure," Jeff said.

"I remember sleeping over here when we were little," Amy said, adding cream and sugar to her coffee. "Grandma Pearl used to make a big breakfast too. Sometimes I forget that she's not with us anymore."

"Me too." Tracy set the plates on the counter and then reached for the silverware drawer. "Thankfully, her presence is felt in all the things she left for us." Tracy's phone dinged, and she grabbed several forks before she reached for her phone. Her eyes grew wide. "Amy!"

"What?" Amy asked, a little startled by her sister's excited tone.

"Tawny thinks she found the veil!"

Amy hurried over to Tracy's side to read the text.

I'm almost positive I've found your veil! Can you and Amy stop by this afternoon to take a look?

"What do you think?" Tracy asked. "Can you meet me there after school?"

"Are you kidding?" Amy tried not to let herself get too excited. What if it wasn't the right veil? "I wish I could go there now, but I need to stop by and pick up Colton and Natalie before I head to school. I don't have time."

"Let's meet there at three thirty," Tracy said. "I'll wait out in the parking lot if I get there early, so we can go in together."

Amy smiled. "Sounds great."

The day felt like it dragged on from there. Between waiting until three thirty to go to the historical society to see the veil and wondering how Miles's first day was going with Stephanie, Amy was distracted and edgy. Every time she looked at the clock, it felt like it wasn't moving.

When the last bell finally rang, Amy had all her stuff gathered and ready to go. She hoped and prayed the kids would get to her room in record time so they could head over to the historical society.

The last one to wander into her room was Colton, who never seemed to be in a hurry.

"We're going to make a stop at the historical society before we head home," Amy told them. "Colton and Natalie, have you been there before?"

Both shook their heads.

"We go all the time," Jana said in a matter-of-fact voice. "My mom likes it there."

Amy smiled to herself as she led the kids to her car.

"Museums are boring," Colton said, to no one in particular.

"Not this one," Matt assured him.

Amy had mentioned to Miles that she and the kids wouldn't be home right away, so she knew he wouldn't be expecting them. She was anxious to get home and hear about his day, but that could wait. All she wanted was to know if the veil Tawny had found was her family veil, or if it was a false alarm.

It was starting to snow when Amy turned into the historical society parking lot. Tracy waited in her car, just like she'd promised.

"Are you excited?" Tracy asked when they were out of their vehicles.

"I'm apprehensive," Amy admitted. "I don't want to get my hopes up."

"Same here."

Tracy said hi to the kids, and their little group trekked into the museum.

"Hello," Tawny called out to them as soon as they entered.

"Whoa," Colton said when he saw an antique plow on display near the front door. "That's cool."

"Want to see the rest of the exhibits?" Matt asked, looking excited to prove to Colton that it wasn't boring.

"Sure."

"Be careful," Amy told her boys. "And don't touch anything."

"I want to show Natalie the exhibit with the old-fashioned kids' things," Jana told Amy.

"Okay, but be careful."

Jana took Natalie by the hand, and the two girls skipped off. Thankfully, the museum wasn't too large and it would be easy to keep track of the kids.

"Well?" Tracy asked Tawny excitedly. "Do you have the veil?"

Tawny nodded and smiled. "I think it's yours—I hope it's yours."

She went to her desk and picked up a gray, acid-free box. "All these boxes are the same. I think I must have overlooked this one when I was searching for it the first time."

Tawny brought it to the counter and slowly lifted the lid. Tissue paper covered the veil, but when Tawny removed it, Amy let out a cry of relief and delight.

"It's the veil!" she said, tears coming to her eyes. "You found it."

The veil was delicate and old, but it had been attended to with such care, it looked practically new.

Amy lifted it out of the box and held it reverently. The pearl headdress was in perfect condition and would match her gown flawlessly.

"I'm so relieved," Tawny said. "I finally tracked down the last board member I was looking for. She served on the board five years ago, during the bridal show, but moved out of state soon after. It took a little prompting, but she was able to finally remember what happened to the veil. She said she put it in the archival room until Pearl could stop by and pick it up, but then she moved away and assumed it was taken care of. Apparently, your grandmother forgot about it."

Tracy wiped away her tears. "See, I knew we'd find it! I didn't give up hope."

"That's because you're stubborn," Amy teased, sniffing away her own tears.

"I'm so happy we found it," Tawny said. "I feel just as excited as you two, I think."

"Thank you so much, Tawny," Amy said. "I can't tell you what this means to me."

Tawny waved her hand. "You don't need to. I already know."

Amy gently laid the veil in the box and patted it one last time. She was going to get to wear her family's veil after all. She'd envisioned it all her life and taken for granted that it would be there for her, but over the past few days she'd been reminded that nothing was guaranteed or certain and everything should be appreciated.

It took a little bit of wrangling, but she was able to get all the kids together.

"Did you find it?" Natalie asked Amy, her eyes wide with curiosity.

"Yes," Amy said with a grin. "We found the veil."

"Yay!" the girls cheered.

"Now we get to wear it too," Jana told Natalie.

Colton and Matt frowned at all the excitement, but neither one asked what was making everyone so happy.

Soon they were on their way out of the museum with the veil safely inside the box in Amy's hands. "I'm not letting this veil out of my sight from now until the wedding," she teased, though she was half-serious.

"I don't blame you," Tracy said. "And when the wedding is done, I'll put it back in the attic with a note on the box threatening anyone who removes it from the attic again—unless they need it for their wedding."

Amy laughed, feeling lighthearted for the first time in weeks.

She was five days away from her wedding, she'd sold her house and moved everything in with Miles, and she had all her vendors secure.

She just prayed that nothing else would go wrong.

Chapter Fifteen

As Amy pulled up to Miles's house, she noticed the glass company van parked in Beverly's driveway. Two men were working on the window while Beverly stood outside in a thick winter coat, her arms crossed, watching them. She didn't seem to notice Amy's arrival.

But the second the kids jumped out of the car, slamming the doors, Beverly spun on her heels and glared at them.

Moppet began to bark and jump around, and Beverly reached down and scooped her up.

Thankfully, the kids didn't seem to notice the irritated neighbor. They ran into the house, their excited chatter seeping into the backyard.

By the time Amy entered through the back door and into the kitchen, Miles had already been told about the wedding veil.

"It's the right veil?" he asked, his eyebrows tilted high with hope and expectancy.

Amy nodded, so excited she could hardly contain herself. He'd been cutting apples for the kids' after-school snack, but he set down the knife and opened his arms to her.

She hugged him tight. "I'm so happy, Miles. I can't tell you what this means to me."

"It's something that connects all the women in your family together. I'm sure, in a way, it makes you feel like they'll all be there with us on our wedding day."

"Yes." Amy loved that he understood. "It's something tangible that connects the past to the present—and the future. Natalie and Jana are already dreaming about wearing it one day, just like I did when I was their age."

"Whoa," Miles said with a protective chuckle as he pulled away. "I'm not ready to start that conversation."

Amy grinned at him.

"Can I see it?" he asked.

"Not until our wedding day. It's bad luck."

"I thought that was only for the dress."

Amy laughed and shrugged. "Who wants to take a chance?" She didn't believe in superstitions, but it was a time-honored tradition she wasn't going to break.

Miles finished cutting the apples, and Amy put peanut butter in four small bowls for the kids to dip them into. When they were finished, the girls said they were going to play dress-up in their bedroom and the boys said they had homework to do.

"When you're done with your homework," Miles said to the boys, "I have a job for you."

"Ah, Dad," Colton protested.

Matt didn't complain out loud, but Amy saw the disappointment in his eyes.

"There are a lot of empty boxes stacking up out in the garage," Miles told them. "I'm going to take them to the recycling center, but they need to be broken down first."

"Can't the girls help us?" Colton asked.

"If I remember correctly, you two have an expensive window to pay for," Miles said. "I haven't gotten the bill yet, but the glass men are at Mrs. Brady's house right now, installing the new window. I'm sure she'll bring it over here soon."

The boys dipped their chins and looked at the ground. Then they marched up the stairs without another word.

"Come find me when you're done with your homework," Miles called after them.

"I'm nervous about that bill," Amy said as she put the dirty dishes in the dishwasher and pushed Scrappy away when he tried to lick the silverware. "I'm sure Beverly didn't spare any expense in having the glass replaced."

"I have a feeling you're right." Miles finished wiping down the table and leaned against the counter. "But I don't blame her for being angry."

"Neither do I." Amy closed the dishwasher and washed her hands.

"What do you feel like doing tonight?" Miles asked her. "More unpacking? Relaxing? Is there something we need to do for the wedding?"

Amy thought through her list. "The place cards are done," she said, thankful Tracy had talked her into asking the others to help her the day before. "Almost everything else that needs to be done can't be done until the day before or the day of the wedding."

"Does that mean we can take the night off?" He wiggled his eyebrows. "Maybe cuddle on the couch and watch a movie?"

"Like last time, when we both slept through it?"

Miles laughed. "At least it was relaxing."

Amy leaned down and picked up Scrappy. She didn't want to bring up Stephanie's name, for fear that Miles would think she was jealous. But she also didn't want to not talk about it. Maybe there was a way to ease into the conversation.

"How was work today?" she asked him as she pet the puppy.

He studied her for a second and smiled. "You can ask me what you want to ask me, Amy. I don't ever want any topic to be off-limits between us. No matter how uncomfortable it might make us feel, I want to talk about everything."

She felt her cheeks growing warm. He knew her better than she gave him credit for.

"Did you see Stephanie today?"

Miles nodded. "Unfortunately, I did. And despite the fact that I told her I didn't want her to come around me at work, she found me in the break room right away this morning when I was getting a cup of coffee. Every time I turned around, she was there. She used the pretense of asking for help and advice, but there were a lot of other people who could have given it to her."

"Did you tell her to leave you alone?"

"I did, multiple times. People don't often think of harassment charges being made against a woman, but I warned her today that if she doesn't leave me alone, that's exactly what I'm going to do."

"I'm sorry, Miles."

He sighed and shook his head. "I asked her again if she was the one who canceled our wedding vendors, but she adamantly denied it."

"Do you believe her?"

"Actually, I do. Part of the reason I believe her is because I asked her how she got your phone number and she told me that Carol gave it to her the day she texted you. I called Carol, and she was able to confirm it. Carol said that she doesn't usually give her clients' phone numbers to each other, but Stephanie told her that she had some questions for you and thought it would be easiest to address them without a go-between. Carol was worried that we were upset about it, but I told her not to be."

"But that doesn't mean she didn't call the vendors."

"No, but I asked Stephanie today if she bought your house because she knew you were my fiancée. She claims she had no idea I was even engaged until after she signed the purchase agreement and Carol told her about us."

"And that was after the vendors had been canceled and rescheduled by Mercy."

"Exactly."

"So it's probably safe to say that Stephanie isn't our culprit—which still leaves Beverly and Mercy."

"That's what I was thinking."

Even if Stephanie didn't cancel their wedding vendors, it didn't mean she wasn't a threat. She'd proven to both Amy and Miles that she wanted them apart.

"Do you think she'll listen and stop bothering you?" Amy asked.

"I sure hope so. When I threatened to turn her in to human resources if she didn't leave me alone, that was right after lunch. I didn't see her again for the rest of the day." He moved away from the counter and put his hands on Amy's arms. "You have nothing to worry about, Amy. I promise you. I will be faithful to you every day of my life."

"I know." She sighed. "It's Stephanie that worries me."

"She's harmless," he reassured her, laying his hand on Scrappy's furry head. "Maybe a little misguided and vindictive, but she's not going to do anything to hurt you or me. And I won't let her do anything to hurt our wedding or life together either."

Amy hoped he was right because she had a sinking feeling that Stephanie had come back to claim Miles and she wasn't going to let anything stop her. Maybe she hadn't been the one to cancel all the wedding vendors, but moving across the country in hopes of being reunited with Miles wasn't something to take lightly.

Amy glanced out the window several times as she and Miles continued to sort and organize boxes that afternoon. The new window at Beverly's house was gorgeous. It was a picture of a fruit bowl, and it sparkled, despite the gray clouds and falling snow, displaying beautiful, bright colors. Purple grapes, red apples, yellow bananas, and green pears were clear to see from where Amy stood. She couldn't help but admire it, though it increased her apprehension about the price tag. Thankfully, she had the extra money from the sale of her furniture to Stephanie, so they wouldn't need to tap into a savings account, but it would still be a painful check to write.

The boys finished their homework and begrudgingly went to the garage with Miles to get their instructions. Dozens of moving boxes had been emptied and waited for them. When Miles came back into the house, Amy was in the kitchen, cutting up carrots. With the cold, stormy weather, she had been craving chicken dumpling soup.

"They'll probably be busy out there until suppertime," Miles said with a smile. "When I left them, they were just realizing that it's fun to break down a cardboard box and isn't hard work at all. I'm sure they won't be complaining too much when they come in."

"As long as they don't find a way to get into more trouble," Amy said, glancing out the window to the detached garage. It was an old carriage house with a second story. When Miles was in high school, he and his brothers had turned the upstairs into a hangout with a television, small refrigerator, and some old couches. Miles now used it as a workout room.

"I'm almost certain they will." Miles laughed. "What good is it to be a boy without trouble?"

Amy rolled her eyes, set aside the carrots, and got out the chicken she'd boiled over the weekend. She was so glad that Matt and Jana would have Miles in their life. He added a perspective that she would never have.

"Want some help?" he asked.

"Sure. Would you like to cut up the celery?"

"Absolutely."

They worked side by side, sharing bits and pieces of their day together. Amy told him about the kids in her classroom, and he told her about one of his coworker's recent trips to Cancun.

"I can't wait to plan a family vacation," Amy said. "I'm looking forward to our little getaway to Quincy next weekend, but won't it be fun to take the kids somewhere warm next winter? Or maybe to Disneyworld this summer?"

"We've been so busy planning our wedding and getting your house ready to sell, we haven't talked about vacations or the fun stuff."

"I like talking about the fun stuff with you." It was exciting to dream with Miles.

As they chatted about possible vacation ideas, Amy glanced out the window and saw Beverly leaving her back door with Moppet in her arms.

She didn't say anything to Miles for a couple of seconds, not sure if Beverly was just stepping out to let the dog go to the bathroom or if she was leaving her house to go on an errand.

When Beverly didn't stop to put down Moppet and didn't head to her garage to get into her car, Amy's pulse started to beat faster.

"Uh, oh," she said.

"What?"

"It looks like we're about to be visited by Beverly. She has an envelope in her hand, which probably means she's coming over with the bill."

Miles groaned. "I'm trying to brace myself, but I don't think I'll be prepared, no matter how hard I try."

Amy had started to make the dumplings, so she wiped the flour off her hands and set the half-prepared dough aside as Beverly passed under the back kitchen window.

Miles went to the door and opened it before Beverly had a chance to knock.

"Come on in, Mrs. Brady."

She entered the kitchen with Moppet under her arm, her expression hard to read.

Scrappy immediately began to bark, which caused Moppet to bark.

"Can't you put that thing away?" Beverly asked with disgust.

Amy chased Scrappy around the kitchen until she cornered him and then grabbed him and his crate. She put him inside and put the crate in the butler's pantry, where Scrappy quieted.

When she reentered the kitchen, she tried to smile at Beverly. "How are you?"

"How am I? Still mourning the loss of my window, though I can't deny I'm pleased with the new one. Have you seen it?"

"I've been admiring it all afternoon," Amy said. "It's lovely."

"It wasn't easy to find, and when I did, I had to have it express-mailed to me from Maine." She pursed her lips together and lifted her eyebrow. "That was one expensive game of hockey your boys played."

Amy inhaled a deep breath, trying to brace herself as Miles had said.

"Is that the bill?" Miles asked.

"Yes." Beverly gave it to him. "You'll find it's itemized, so there shouldn't be any questions."

"We trust you've been fair."

Beverly shifted uncomfortably.

Upstairs, the girls were playing, and something loud hit the floor. Beverly jumped, and Moppet barked.

"We're okay," one of the girls called down.

"My nerves," Beverly said, touching her temple. "I don't know how you can stand all that noise. Moppet is trembling violently."

"You get used to it," Amy said. "I'm a first-grade teacher, so I listen to it all day long. The only thing I worry about is someone getting hurt."

"How dreadful for you," Beverly said. "What an awful profession to go into."

"Someone has to do it," Amy said. "Where would any of us be without our first-grade teachers? It's very rewarding."

Beverly didn't look convinced. Instead, she lifted her chin. "The wedding is this weekend?"

"Yes," Miles said, glancing at Amy. "If you'd like to come—"

"Heavens, no," she said. "My nephew is getting married the same day. I'll be busy at his wedding."

"Oh?" Amy asked. "Is that Mercy Fellbaum's wedding?"

Beverly frowned. "Do you know Mercy?"

"I met her at Whimsy." Amy's pulse ticked higher. Perhaps now was a good time to confront Beverly about her possible involvement in canceling their wedding vendors. "I—"

A cell phone began to ring, but it wasn't Miles's or Amy's.

Moppet began to bark again.

"Oh dear," Beverly said as she adjusted Moppet in her arms. "Hush, sweetheart. Hush." She pulled her phone out of her pocket and looked at it. Amy couldn't help but notice Mercy's name on the screen in big, bold letters.

"Oh my," Beverly said, fumbling to turn off the ringer as Moppet continued to bark in a high, sharp tone. She managed to press a button to silence the call, but then Amy heard Mercy saying hello.

Beverly put the phone to her ear. "Hello? Hello? Oh hello, dear. I can't talk." She looked up at Amy and then Miles and turned her back to them. "I'll call you later. Goodbye."

Amy glanced at Miles, and he nodded, as if letting her know that he'd seen the name too.

"I must go," Beverly said. "I expect to be paid as soon as possible for the window. I have incurred debts that I cannot afford on my fixed income."

"I can get my checkbook now," Miles said as he moved to the stairs.

"That won't be necessary." She appeared in a big hurry all of a sudden. "I can't get to the bank until tomorrow anyway. Bring it by sometime tomorrow. That will be soon enough." She walked toward the door.

Miles had to move aside for her. She didn't say goodbye as she let herself out.

But that didn't stop Amy and Miles from calling goodbye to her.

When the door had closed, Miles turned to Amy.

"What do you think about that?" he asked. "Did you see Mercy's name on the phone?"

"I did. And Beverly didn't seem to want to talk to her in front of us. I was just about to confront her about canceling our wedding vendors when Mercy called."

"If they're the ones who are sabotaging our wedding, I'm not surprised. Beverly acted very suspiciously."

"I just wish I had thought to call the number Trish gave me. I want to see if Beverly is the one who called our vendors."

"We'll have to find another reason to visit her," Miles suggested. "We can come up with something."

Amy glanced at the envelope in his hand. "Are you ready to take a look?"

Miles opened the seal and pulled out the piece of paper inside while Amy stood next to him.

Even though she had been trying to prepare herself for the cost, it was still a surprise. Amy sucked in her breath.

"Ouch," Miles said.

"Yeah."

"Was it what you expected?"

Amy shook her head. "I didn't think it would be that much."

"I was thinking it would be in this ballpark, especially seeing how quickly she had it installed. I'm sure everything was rushed, since she knew we'd be paying for it."

"It looks like the boys will be working for a long, long time to pay for this one."

"It's a good lesson to learn," Miles said. "Hardship often teaches us the most."

"We'll need to be creative to find jobs for them outside of their regular chores."

The soup began to boil over, so Amy rushed to remove the lid.

The bill from Beverly wasn't ideal, but she was thankful they had the resources to take care of it. Not everything was as easy to handle.

Chapter Sixteen

$\mathcal{S}$chool went smoother on Tuesday, since Amy didn't have the question of the veil distracting her. She still couldn't believe she had it in her possession. She'd brought it to Tracy's with her the night before after she, Matt, and Jana had left Miles's house. It was airing out in the guest closet, hanging next to her wedding gown. Amy had stood for a long time and just looked at the dress and veil the night before, marveling that she would wear them Saturday as she became Miles's wife.

"Miss Allen?" One of Amy's students raised her hand.

"Yes, Charity. What is it?" The class was working on some math problems, and Amy expected her to have a question about one of them.

"What will we call you after you get married?"

Several of the other children looked up at Amy, questions in their gazes.

Amy had told them she was getting married to Dr. Anderson. Some of them knew him from being his patients. She was taking Friday and the following Monday off from school, so she had been preparing them for a substitute teacher, but no one had yet asked her what they should call her when she came back.

"Do we call you Dr. Anderson too?" Jake asked with a frown.

"No." Amy chuckled to herself. "But that's a good question. I'll be Mrs. Anderson when I come back to school next Tuesday."

The kids took a few seconds to process that information.

"Okay," she said, looking at the clock over the door. "The lunch bell will ring in about five minutes, and we need to wrap up our math class before then."

Everyone quickly finished their worksheets, and Amy gathered them as the kids prepared for lunch. After she walked them to the cafeteria, she returned to her empty classroom and pulled out the lunch she'd brought with her that day. Sometimes she went to the faculty lounge to eat with the other teachers, but today she wanted to look over her RSVP list, since she needed to get the final count to the caterer by one o'clock.

Amy ate her salad while she opened her email to see if she'd gotten any last-minute RSVPs. She was just about to click on the caterer's email address with the head count when her cell phone rang.

It was Les Trois Colombes, which surprised Amy. She pressed the green icon and smiled. "Hello," she said. "I was just about to email you."

"Is this Amy Allen?" the man on the other end of the phone said, his tone a bit harsh.

"Yes. As I said, I was just about to email you with the final head count."

There was a pause on the other end.

Amy frowned. "Is there a problem?"

"Yes, actually, there is. We have a signed contract, Ms. Allen, which means something to us."

"I know," Amy said, her pulse jumping. "What's the trouble?"

"If you cancel now, we have the right to retain your deposit."

"I'm not canceling," Amy said, trying to keep her voice calm. "I said I was just about to send you my final head count. I have until one o'clock today, don't I?" She glanced at the clock. Maybe he was upset because she'd gotten the date and time wrong and should have responded earlier.

"You're not canceling?" the man asked.

"No, of course not. My wedding is on Saturday. Who am I speaking to?"

"The manager of Les Trois Colombes, Louis Cadott. I have a note here, taken from one of my staff yesterday, telling me that you called to cancel your order. Is this a mistake?"

Amy stood, her heart pounding. "Yes, that's a mistake. I didn't call to cancel. I am very much planning to have your restaurant cater my wedding reception."

"Oh, good," he said, relief evident in his sigh. "I was hoping it was a mistake."

"Please," she said, "if anyone else calls to try to cancel, disregard them and let me know." She quickly explained how this had happened before. "I don't know who is doing this, but I'm going to get to the bottom of it today."

"You will email me the final head count?" he asked.

"Yes. I will do that immediately, and then I'll call all my other vendors to confirm with them as well."

"Thank you, Ms. Allen. I am sorry for this inconvenience."

Not as sorry as Amy was.

"That's okay. It's not your fault. Do you happen to have a phone number for the person who called?"

"No, I'm afraid not. It would be almost impossible to track. We receive many calls a day, and I do not know when this one came in."

"All right. Thank you anyway."

Amy ended the call and immediately sent the restaurant the details they would need though her mind spun with all sorts of possibilities and worry about the other vendors. Had her wedding saboteur struck again? And if so, who else had they called?

After finishing the email, Amy pulled out her wedding binder and found the number for the Museum of Wonder. When Elaine Hartford answered, Amy was almost too nervous to speak.

"Hello, Elaine," she said. "This is Amy Allen."

"Hello, Amy. I was just going to call you."

Amy closed her eyes as she braced for the news.

"We have a question about where you want the head table to sit in the hall. It's not a huge deal, but I know you want to get in here on Friday to decorate, and I wanted to make the day as smooth as possible for you."

Amy let out a sigh of relief. "Have you had anyone call to cancel our reservation?"

There was a slight pause. "No. Is someone planning to do that?"

"No." Amy's voice was firm. "You remember what I told you about our original plans and how someone canceled them?"

"Yes, of course."

"Well, someone tried it again with our second caterer. I'm going to call everyone on my list and tell them to be on the lookout for a phone call like that. If you should happen to get one, please keep track of the number and let me know immediately."

"Of course. I'm happy to help." She paused and then said, "Now, about that head table."

Amy answered her questions and then ended the call, eager to get in touch with her other vendors.

Thankfully, no one else had received a phone call from the saboteur, and all of them were on the lookout now.

The lunch that Amy brought still sat half-eaten on her desk. She'd lost the little appetite she'd had.

Had Mercy or Beverly called Les Trois Colombes? Until she'd met Mercy and talked to her, she'd assumed she had done it the first time to steal all of Amy's vendors. Now she suspected Beverly was the one behind it and had used Mercy as an unwitting accomplice. Was Beverly at it again?

It was time to confront Beverly once and for all to put a stop to this nonsense.

Amy rarely called Miles at work, but she wanted him to know what had happened. She dialed his cell phone, not expecting to speak to him right away, since he was probably with a patient.

She was surprised when he answered.

"Hello, Amy," he said with a smile in his voice. "To what do I owe this lovely surprise?"

Amy couldn't help but smile, though she was still upset about the restaurant. "I'm happy I reached you. I thought you'd be busy."

"I'm on my lunch break."

"Of course." Amy took a deep breath and told him about the restaurant.

"This is getting ridiculous," he said.

"I agree. And I'm tired of worrying about it. I called all of our vendors to have them keep a lookout, but they're probably tired of it too."

"We need to put a stop to this."

"I almost forgot. You have a staff meeting after work this afternoon, don't you?"

"Yes. Hopefully, it won't last more than an hour. We can go over to Beverly's when I get home."

"Okay. I'm planning to stop by Whimsy again this afternoon and talk to Mercy. She seemed innocent, but I want to make sure. I'm going to ask her point-blank if she's the one responsible for this mess."

Miles sighed. "I'm sorry this is happening, Amy. You have more important things to worry about right now."

The recess bell rang, which meant that Amy only had twenty minutes left before her students would be back in class. She needed to prep for language arts next.

"I should get going, Miles," she said. "I'll talk to you later. I love you."

"I love you too. See you after work."

She didn't have long to sit and mull over what she planned to say to Mercy later that afternoon. The bell waited for no one, and the kids would return before she knew it.

"Thank you for meeting me here," Amy said to Tracy a few hours later as she stepped out of her car in the Whimsy parking lot. She had dropped the kids off at home and called Tracy to see if she could meet her to confront Mercy.

"I'm happy I was free," Tracy said. She shut her car door and shuffled over to Amy.

The snow still fell in bits and spurts, sometimes in mixed precipitation, which left the sidewalks and roadways slippery.

"Have you checked the weather forecast recently?" Tracy asked as they walked toward the store together.

"No. I haven't had a chance. Why?"

Tracy pressed her lips together and frowned. "It's not looking great for this weekend. They've extended the winter weather advisory through Sunday now. We could end up getting a lot of snow out of this front."

"Sunday?" Amy sighed. "Can't this wedding catch a break?"

"We found the veil, didn't we?" Tracy reminded her. "I know it doesn't make the other things easier, but at least it's something."

"You're right," Amy said. "It's something. I just need to keep focusing on the positive."

"Are you ready to face Mercy again?"

"Yes, and I'm planning to be a lot firmer with her this time."

"I've got your back," Tracy said with a decisive nod.

Amy opened the door, and her nose was greeted by the overwhelming aroma of candles.

"Hello," Pammy said, glancing up from arranging a display near the front door. "Welcome back to Whimsy. How are you enjoying that clock?"

Amy had almost forgotten about the clock. "I love it. It fit perfectly on the wall I had planned for it."

"Wonderful. We have a few more pieces in that collection, if you'd like to see them. There are some shelves and candle holders that match it too."

"Not at the moment," Amy said, trying to look around the store without appearing too eager. "Is Mercy working today?"

"She is." Pammy pointed toward the back of the store. "I think she's stocking inventory in the household department."

"Thank you."

Amy and Tracy left Pammy and wove their way through the store. It was hard not to get distracted by all the beautiful items for sale. Amy had to pull Tracy along when she stopped at a display of cookbooks and stoneware.

Finally, they found Mercy. She was stocking a shelf of bathroom accessories. She glanced up and blinked several times before she appeared to remember who Amy and Tracy were.

"Hello," she said, though her greeting wasn't as warm and welcoming as last time. No doubt she was a little leerier than before.

"Hi," Amy said, trying not to get too upset, though she was tired of this game someone was playing with her and her wedding.

"What can I do for you?" Mercy asked.

"I'm going to cut to the chase," Amy said. "I still haven't figured out who canceled all my wedding vendors. But whoever it is hasn't given up. Someone called my new caterer and tried to cancel my order. Thankfully, I was able to speak to them before too much damage was done, but I'm tired, and I want to know, once and for all, who is trying to make my life more difficult."

Mercy lifted her hands and shrugged, her face filled with concern and empathy. "I'm sorry. I wish I could help you."

"Was it you?" Tracy asked, sounding just as fed up as Amy.

"No." Mercy shook her head. "I have no idea who would do something like this. All I did was call the vendors that my fiancé's aunt recommended."

"And that aunt is Beverly Brady, correct?" Amy asked.

Mercy nodded. "Yes. She gave me a list of places to call, and they were all available. Since I'm not from Canton, I didn't know which vendors to use. It was a godsend for her to help me."

Amy glanced at Tracy and shook her head. Then she looked back at Mercy. "Beverly is my fiancé's next-door neighbor, and she's been very upset about our upcoming wedding. She doesn't like the noise and chaos of extra children in the neighborhood either. She's made it very clear that she wishes we weren't getting married and that I wasn't moving in with my children."

Mercy looked genuinely surprised. "I'm sorry to hear that. I don't know Beverly that well and have only seen her at a few family events. She's always been very pleasant to me. I wasn't aware of her treatment of you and your family."

Amy believed Mercy. She could see that Mercy was the innocent bystander in this situation.

"I have the list she made for me," Mercy said. "I don't want to get her in trouble, but if it's helpful, I can give it to you."

"Do you have it here?" Amy asked.

"Yes. I have a folder of information for my wedding, and I brought it to work with me today. I'll get it for you."

She walked away from Amy and Tracy, leaving them alone.

"Do you think she's innocent?" Tracy asked.

"Yes." Amy nodded and took a deep breath. "I think Beverly's our culprit."

"Did you see her cell phone in her work apron?"

Amy shook her head. "I wasn't paying attention."

"I can call the number that Trish gave you when Mercy comes back, and if her phone doesn't ring, it's probably safe to say she's not guilty."

"Except she might not have the ringer on while she's working," Amy said.

Tracy waved her hand. "We might as well try."

Amy texted the number to Tracy's phone, and Tracy stepped away, as if she was taking a phone call.

"Here," Mercy said, handing the handwritten note to Amy. "This is what Beverly gave me a few weeks ago."

Amy took the paper. It was similar to the page she had seen by Beverly's phone the day she'd stopped by to give her cookies. There was a design on the top with a sunflower. If it had come from the same notepad, Amy would be able to compare them when she stopped by Beverly's later with Miles.

Tracy stood behind Mercy, and when Amy glanced in her direction, she held up her phone and shook her head, which meant that she was calling the number but Mercy's phone wasn't ringing.

"Thank you," Amy said. She folded the note and put it into her coat pocket.

"Please don't tell Beverly I gave you that. She's the only family I'll have in Canton when Paul is in Japan this spring, and I don't want to alienate her."

"I won't tell her." Amy understood the importance of family, even if they were difficult sometimes.

"Thank you," Mercy said. "Again, I'm so sorry about what happened."

"I am too."

Tracy joined Amy again, and they said goodbye to Mercy.

"It looks like you know who tried to sabotage your wedding," Tracy said when they stood in the snow beside their cars a few minutes later.

"But now we need to prove it."

"What do you plan to do?"

"Miles and I need to give her a check for the window, and we're planning to do it this evening after he gets home from work. Her notepad is on a little desk right inside her back door. I'll look to see if it matches the paper from the list Mercy gave me, and then I'll call the number and see if Beverly's phone rings. I think that's enough evidence to confront her with the accusation. Hopefully, once she knows that we know, she'll stop trying to ruin things for us."

"I'll be praying for you," Tracy said. "And waiting to hear what happens when you come by tonight."

"Thanks, Tracy. I appreciate all your help and support."

"You're welcome. I'll talk to you later." Tracy got into her car and waved as she drove away.

Amy got into her car, but she sat in the parking lot for a few minutes to take some deep breaths before she turned on her engine and left Whimsy.

The roads were slick, so she took her time driving toward Miles's house—though she caught her thoughts and tried to think of it as her house too. How long would it take for her to consider it home?

She had unpacked at least half their boxes, though there were still many left to go. Would that make her feel like it was home? Or would it be the wedding and sleeping there full-time that would finally do it?

She contemplated this question as she pulled up to the house and parked near the garage. Large snowflakes fell, making the world feel like a snow globe. Everything was peaceful and calm—until her gaze landed on Beverly's house.

Any peace that Amy felt was gone as she thought about the encounter she and Miles would have that evening. Part of her wanted to get it over with, and the other part wished she didn't have to go at all. But if it meant putting a stop to the wedding sabotage, she would do whatever it would take.

She just hoped they had found their culprit.

Chapter Seventeen

I'm home," Amy called out as she entered the kitchen, smiling at the sound of the word *home* on her lips. Maybe it wouldn't take too long after all. "Where is everyone?"

The house was quiet—too quiet. It wasn't the first time Amy thought it would be a good idea to have some kind of intercom system. Maybe they could install one and Amy could just press a button and speak to everyone in the house at the same time. If the boys ended up sleeping on the third floor, they would definitely need to get something to communicate between the main floor and the attic. A speaking tube had originally been built into the walls, connecting the ground floor to the bedrooms, but someone had cut the tube at some point, probably remodeling, and it no longer worked.

"Hello," Amy called again as she took off her coat and hung it on the hook near the door.

Still, nothing. Even Scrappy was nowhere to be seen or heard.

Her pulse picked up speed as she called up the back steps. Had it been a mistake to leave the kids alone? She walked into the dining room to call out there.

"Hi Mom," Jana said, poking her head out of the family room. "Natalie and I are watching *Frozen*."

Relief flooded Amy. "Do you know where the boys are?"

Jana shrugged.

"Is Scrappy with you."

"Yep!"

"Do you or Natalie have any homework?"

"Nope." Jana grinned.

"Okay, but after *Frozen* ends, I want the TV off for the night, okay? There are some chores to do."

"You got it," Jana said in a long, drawn-out voice as she ran back into the family room.

"Boys," Amy called from the bottom of the front stairs.

"What?" Matt called.

"Just checking to see where you are. Is Colton up there?"

"Yeah, he's in his room."

"Okay. After you get your homework done, I want you two to get the recycling organized."

"Ah, Mom," Matt groaned.

The doorbell rang, startling Amy. She wasn't expecting anyone.

A sheer curtain hung over the glass interior door, distorting the new arrival outside the exterior door. Amy could tell it was a woman but wasn't sure who.

She opened the interior door and stepped into the entryway—and that's when she saw who had come to visit. But perhaps *visit* wasn't the right word. Amy had a feeling that this person had come to cause trouble.

"Hello, Stephanie," she said as she opened the heavy exterior door. Stephanie looked attractive and fashionable. She was probably one of the best-dressed women in Canton. Her hair appeared freshly curled, though she had probably been at work all day, her makeup was still bright, and her nails were perfectly manicured. Her clothing looked expensive, as did her purse. Everything was in its place.

"Annie." Stephanie seemed surprised to see Amy standing there. "I had no idea you'd be here."

"It's Amy," she said, trying to be patient. "And I'm not sure why you're surprised. Miles and I will be married in a few days."

"Someone told me you were staying at your sister's house until the wedding."

"I'm sleeping there," Amy said, but then she realized she didn't want to give Stephanie more information than necessary. "What can I do for you?"

"I'm here to see Miles on a—" She paused and leaned forward, dropping her voice. "A personal matter."

"He's still at the staff meeting. I'm surprised you're not."

"I just left there and thought Miles would be home by now." She frowned, as if curious and concerned. "I wonder where he could be. He told me he was coming right home."

Colton came down the steps but paused on the last stair.

"Do you remember me, Colton?" Stephanie asked with a hopeful lilt to her voice. "You've grown into such a handsome young man. You look just like your daddy. Don't follow in his footsteps and be a heartbreaker like him."

"Colton," Amy said, "why don't you go to the kitchen and get a snack ready for everyone. I'm sure they're hungry. There are some baby carrots and ranch dressing in the fridge."

Colton frowned at Stephanie and then walked toward the kitchen. Amy couldn't be sure if he remembered her or not.

"What a good-looking kid," Stephanie said as she stepped over the threshold and into the vestibule.

Amy took a step back, surprised Stephanie would come in without being invited.

Stephanie took off her coat and draped it over her arm. "I'll wait for Miles. Feel free to return to whatever it was you were doing, Ally."

"Amy," she said again, though this time she said it through clenched teeth.

Stephanie laughed and shook her head. "I don't know why I can't remember your name. It's so common and simple."

The insult was intentional, Amy was certain. "I don't think Miles will be happy to see you here," she said. "Didn't he tell you to leave him alone?"

Stephanie frowned and looked around with a raised eyebrow. "What a beautiful home. I'd change everything, of course. It's so old-fashioned, but the bones are good. I'd add in some modern flooring and remove the old wallpaper, not to mention paint the trim a lighter color to add some brightness to the rooms." She walked into the living room, and Amy followed her. "It wouldn't hurt to have some different furniture too. I'm surprised you didn't bring your furniture from the house over here. It would look much better than this old stuff. You can tell Miles doesn't have a woman influencing his home decor."

"He does, actually," Amy said, lifting her chin. "Me."

Stephanie laughed. "Oh, Abby. Don't take it personally. I have a feeling you'll leave your mark here, but Miles needs a woman with a stronger sense of style, don't you think?" She dipped her head. "What is it you do again? Aren't you an elementary school teacher?

That explains how exhausted you look. And then to come home and deal with more children must be mind-numbing. What a tedious existence. I can't imagine that Miles expects to lead an exciting life with you."

Amy's jaw dropped, and she felt her face grow warm. She'd never been more insulted in her life. "I love what I do for a living," she said, her voice rising. "And I love coming home to the kids. It's not mind-numbing or tedious at all."

"Oh, Addy," Stephanie said, placing her manicured hand on Amy's arm. "You're overreacting. I meant no harm. Just making small talk."

"I think you should leave," Amy said. She stepped aside to indicate the front door.

Stephanie's lips thinned, and then she said, "If I'm not mistaken, this is Miles's house. I'll leave when he tells me to."

"I'm telling you to go now," Miles said as he strode into the room.

Amy hadn't even heard him arrive. She'd been so preoccupied with Stephanie, she hadn't noticed anything else.

Miles put his arm around Amy and drew her to his side.

"Miles," Stephanie said. "I was wondering when you'd get here. Andy was just telling me about her work."

"I heard what you said to Amy," he said. "It was rude and insensitive. You can pretend to be innocent, Stephanie, but I know that you came here to intimidate Amy and belittle her. It won't work, because I know something you don't. Amy is one of the kindest, smartest, and strongest women I've ever known. Nothing you could say would diminish her in any way."

Stephanie lifted her chin and pulled back. "How dare you accuse me of being rude and insensitive. I was simply making small talk."

"I also heard you tell Amy that this is my house and that you'd leave when I told you. But this is Amy's house too, and she's asked you to leave. If you don't, I'll call the police, and they won't be as nice to you."

"My goodness," Stephanie said, hugging her coat close to her stomach. "I wouldn't have come here if I thought I would be treated this way."

"Why did you come here?" Amy asked. "Other than to insult me?"

"I came," Stephanie said as she began to put her coat on, "because I thought I could talk some sense into Miles. He won't let me talk to him at work, so I thought maybe he'd be more receptive to me at his house. I can see I was wrong."

"Don't bother to approach me anywhere," Miles said. "At work or at home. This behavior is inappropriate, Stephanie, and I won't hesitate to report you to the authorities if it continues."

"My goodness," she said again as she buttoned up her coat. "What a lot of drama over a little visit." She walked to the front door. "I had mistakenly assumed you would be happy to see me in Canton again, Miles. I can't imagine what I've done to make you so upset."

Miles still had his arm around Amy, and he pulled her a little closer. "You've insulted the woman I love, and you won't take no for an answer. I can list more grievances, if you'd like."

"Don't bother." Stephanie opened the front door and stepped onto the porch. Without saying goodbye, she strode down the steps, onto the sidewalk, and then got into her car and drove away.

Miles closed the door after her.

Amy hadn't realized until now that she was trembling.

"I'm sorry, Amy," Miles said. "No one should have to deal with someone like Stephanie—let alone my fiancée."

"I didn't know what to say to her," Amy said. "I'm shocked that someone would talk to me that way."

"And I'm glad that you're shocked. It only confirms for me that I'm marrying the kindest, sweetest, and most thoughtful woman in the world."

"I'm not the bravest or the strongest," she said.

He embraced her. "It takes a lot of bravery and strength not to lash out at someone who's attacking you like that. You could have returned her insults with some of your own, but you didn't. I'm proud of you."

She laid her cheek against his chest, her nerves beginning to calm. "Thank you."

"I'll say this as much as you need to hear it, but I hope you start to believe it soon." Miles pulled back and met Amy's gaze. "This is your home today, tomorrow, and forever. If you don't want someone to enter this house, tell them so. If you want someone to leave, tell them. If you want to throw open the door and invite everyone in Canton over here, then do it. You don't have to ask permission or seek my approval. This is your home, Amy Allen-soon-to-be-Anderson. Believe it."

Amy smiled at him. "This is my home," she said.

"Good." He hugged her again and sighed. "Now, let's deal with the other unpleasant task for today, and then let's take the night off and do something fun with the kids, okay?"

Amy knew what unpleasant task he was talking about, and she dreaded it almost as much as the thought of facing Stephanie again.

But this time, Miles would be by her side. That thought alone gave her the courage she needed.

Fifteen minutes later, Amy felt herself starting to tremble again as she and Miles left the back door and walked down the porch steps to go to Beverly's house.

"It's okay, Amy," Miles said, taking her hand in his. "Beverly can't do anything more to hurt us or our wedding. All we're going to do is confront her and ask if she canceled our wedding vendors."

"What if she says she didn't do it?"

"We can't force her to confess, but I think it's a good idea to call the number while we're there and see if her phone rings. If it does, then we won't need her confession. We'll know it's her and can tell her to stop interfering."

"I hate confrontation."

"I don't know many people who enjoy it."

"The kids seem to like it."

Miles laughed.

They walked across the driveway to Beverly's back stoop.

Amy took a deep breath and then walked up to the door with Miles at her side.

He smiled at her and winked as he rang the doorbell. "We've got this."

It took a few minutes, but Beverly opened the door, a frown on her face. Moppet was at her feet, barking at Amy and Miles.

"Where is the check, Dr. Anderson? I thought you were going to put it in my mailbox today. Have you come to tell me that you're not paying? Why am I not surprised?"

"I decided to hand-deliver it instead," Miles said. "May we come in?"

Beverly looked behind Amy and Miles, as if gauging the weather. It was cold, and snowflakes still fell from the overcast sky.

"Fine, but make it quick. I have things to do." She stepped aside, allowing Miles and Amy to enter.

It wasn't too unlike Miles and Amy's kitchen. The houses had probably been built around the same time, by the same builder. There were definitely differences, and the styles were not similar, but it had the same layout.

Amy glanced at the notepad as they passed by the desk and saw the same sunflower that was on the note Mercy had given her. It was yet one more confirmation that they had found their saboteur. But why would Beverly do something like that—and how did she think she'd get away with it?

Beverly closed the back door and picked up Moppet. "Why couldn't you simply have handed the check to me and been on your way?"

"Because Amy and I would like to talk to you about something else."

Beverly looked between them, frowning. "What?"

"I would like to know why you tried to sabotage our wedding," Amy said. "Was it to hurt us and prevent us from getting married? Or was it simply to help your nephew and his fiancée, Mercy?"

Beverly stared at them and then said, "I don't know what you're talking about."

"We think you do," Miles said. "Amy saw the list of our vendors on your notepad when she brought cookies here, and we know that someone called all those vendors, pretending to be Amy, to cancel them."

"We also know that Mercy called each of the vendors and rescheduled them for her own wedding just a day or so later."

"Why do you think I would do something like that?" Beverly asked.

"Because Mercy told me that she didn't know any of the vendors in Canton and that you were the one to suggest each one." Amy lifted her chin, remembering that Mercy didn't want her to show Beverly the physical list.

"Again," Beverly said, lifting her shoulder, "just because I made some suggestions doesn't mean I was the one to cancel the vendors."

Amy looked at Miles. This was what she had been afraid of. Beverly wasn't willing to own up to her guilt. There was only one way to find out for sure.

Reaching in her back pocket, Amy pulled out her cell phone. Before they'd come over, she had cued the number up so it was ready to go.

"What are you doing?" Beverly asked.

"I have the phone number of the person who pretended to be me and canceled our orders."

Beverly's eyes opened wide as she looked from Amy's cell phone to the counter where another cell phone sat.

"If I dial this number," Amy said, "will your cell phone ring, Mrs. Brady?"

Beverly stared at Amy for several seconds before she let out a sigh. "Fine," she said, disdain in her voice. "It was me. I called everyone and said I was Amy Allen. I canceled your orders and reservations, and then I gave the list to Mercy. Is that what you want me to say?"

"As long as it's the truth, yes," Amy said. She wished she felt relieved at Beverly's admission, but she didn't.

"It's the truth," Beverly said. "I had no problem doing it either. I've made it very clear that I don't want children living next door. It's a daily inconvenience in my life—so a little inconvenience in yours seemed fitting."

"What if I hadn't learned the truth in time?" Amy asked. "What if I hadn't called the baker to change my order?"

"Oh, don't be so dramatic. You would have figured it out eventually," Beverly said with a roll of her eyes.

"What about Les Trois Colombes?" Amy frowned. "Why did you try to cancel our caterer again?"

"I was angry and frustrated about the window." Beverly pressed her lips together.

"What you did was unkind and childish," Miles said. "You made more work for Amy and added to her stress."

"Just as you and your children have added to mine. Even though I've made my point clear, your family continues to dishonor me and my property. Why must I suffer and no one else?"

"That's not how it is," Miles said. "We're not purposefully causing you trouble, but you deliberately tried to sabotage our wedding. The two are nowhere near the same."

"It doesn't matter," Beverly said. "You're still getting married, and I still have to put up with your children, so I'll continue to suffer while your wedding comes and goes."

"I'm sorry you feel that way," Amy said, "but our home means a great deal to us, and we won't be leaving, so you have a choice to make. You can either learn to live with us, or make everyone's lives more difficult by being unkind and unneighborly."

Beverly looked down at Moppet and didn't meet their gazes.

"How did you know which vendors to call?" Miles asked after a few uncomfortable moments of silence.

"It wasn't difficult in a small town. I just called around to all the likely businesses and told them I was Amy Allen. If they had been secured by Amy, I knew I had the right business. I made a list and gave it to Mercy. She called everyone within the next couple of days." She finally looked up at them. "But she's innocent. She had no idea."

"I've gathered that much," Amy said.

Beverly sighed. "I won't apologize for not liking your family, but perhaps I was a bit vindictive in how I handled my displeasure. I'm sorry I made your life more difficult, Ms. Allen."

Amy was stunned at Beverly's admission and apology. She stared at her for a second before nodding, trying to find her voice. "I appreciate that, Mrs. Brady."

"This doesn't mean I like that you and your children are moving in, and it definitely doesn't mean that I want them anywhere near my property. Thankfully, Moppet's medication seems to be helping her anxiety. I still insist that the children keep their voices down as much as possible. Moppet doesn't do well with the noise, and neither do I."

"We will do our best to honor your wishes," Miles said, "but we make no promises. The children must be free to be children, as long as they are respectful and kind. If you have any problems with them, I will give you our phone numbers, and you may call us."

"And," Amy added, "if you have any emergency, big or small, please feel free to call on us as well."

Beverly's lips parted, and a frown dipped her eyebrows. "Truly? After everything, you'd still be willing to help me if I needed it?"

"Of course," Miles said. "That's what neighbors are for."

Beverly's face smoothed, and she nodded. "Well, I suppose that's acceptable."

Amy glanced at Miles, trying not to smile.

It was a start, however small.

Chapter Eighteen

$\mathcal{I}$t was finally Friday, the day before the wedding. Both Amy and Miles had taken the day off work, though they had sent the kids to school. It would give them time to run errands. They'd gone to the florist and the printer and the grocery store. They'd also visited the courthouse in Monticello, the county seat, for their marriage license. It had been a whirlwind day, dropping some things off at the church, other things at the museum, and still others at home. They had enjoyed a quick lunch in Monticello and were waiting to pick up the kids from school to head back to the Museum of Wonders to start decorating, when it began to snow hard.

"This isn't good," Amy said to Miles on her cell phone. He was in his Jeep behind her in the pick-up line, since they had used both vehicles for all the deliveries.

"No," he said, "but we knew it was coming."

"I hoped it would pass us by. Thankfully, your family is already in town and won't have to travel in this weather."

Miles's mom and dad had arrived the night before and were staying in Colton's room. Colton was temporarily bunking with Matt. They'd enjoyed a meal together soon after their arrival, which Amy had loved. It was fun seeing them back in their old house, surrounded by some of their grandchildren, relishing their retirement. They'd met up with Miles's brothers and their families at the hotel that morning and were spending time with their other grandchildren at the pool. They had brought gifts for all the kids, including Matt and Jana.

"Hopefully our other guests won't have any trouble traveling tomorrow," Miles said as the front doors of the school burst open and children began to pour out. "I'll see you at the museum, Amy."

"Okay, bye." Amy ended the call and watched for the kids. Jana and Natalie came out, arm in arm, just as happy and excited about becoming sisters tomorrow as Amy and Miles were about being married. They ran to Amy's car while Matt and Colton emerged from the school and went to Miles's vehicle.

"It's snowing!" Natalie exclaimed as she jumped in, Jana right behind her. "It's so pretty."

"It is pretty," Amy admitted—though she struggled to find the beauty in it when it hindered her wedding plans.

"We're getting married tomorrow!" Jana said as she pulled the door closed.

"I'm getting married tomorrow," Amy corrected.

"So are we," Jana insisted. "We're going to be a real family tomorrow. Isn't that what marriage means, Mama?"

Amy smiled and nodded. "Yes, I guess you're right. We're all getting married tomorrow."

The girls giggled. Their excitement was so high, it was palpable, and Amy was thankful. It made things easier that they were happy.

She followed the other cars out of the pick-up line and onto the street. Everyone drove at a snail's pace as the snow fell faster and thicker.

Amy turned on her windshield wipers, but the snow was so heavy, it was hard to see down the block.

The cars came to a stop, and Amy waited patiently for them to start moving again, but no one budged. She tried in vain to see what the holdup was but couldn't see anything beyond the cars ahead of her. She would have turned off onto a side street, but she was stuck in the middle of the road.

When the cars finally started to move, she crept past two vehicles that had been in an accident and thanked God that it looked like no one got hurt.

It took longer than normal to get to the museum, but when she did, she saw that several cars were already there. Not only was Miles's family coming to help decorate, but Tracy, Robin, Sara, Jeff, Terry, and Kai were coming too.

When Amy finally parked the car, she pulled her phone out of her purse and checked the weather app. It didn't look good. The snow was supposed to fall all day and night, possibly letting up tomorrow afternoon, right before the wedding at three.

Since there was nothing she could do about it, she put her phone away and tried not to worry.

There were boxes of decorations, grocery bags full of snacks, and totes with place cards, menus, and signs that needed to be hauled into the museum. Amy gave each of the kids something light to carry as she and Miles hefted the bigger boxes and they all headed inside.

"There you are," Tracy said when she met them at the door. "I was beginning to wonder if we'd have to send out a search party."

"Sorry," Amy said as Tracy took the large box of chair covers from her. "There was an accident near the school, and traffic was backed up. I'm sorry that I didn't think to call."

"That's okay," Tracy said. "I know you have a lot on your mind. And we've been busy getting things laid out like you wanted."

The rented tables and chairs had been delivered earlier in the day. Some of Miles's family members were still setting them up and arranging them.

"Perfect. Thank you."

"Are there more boxes in your cars?" Robin asked as she approached.

"Yes."

"Terry and Jeff," Robin called, "we need your help."

Soon, everything was unloaded, and Amy was directing the decorating committee, as they'd affectionately called themselves. Thankfully, Miles's brothers and their wives had known Tracy, Jeff, Robin, and Terry for years. Most of them had gone to school together. Sara was introduced to everyone after she arrived from work, and soon she was busy putting together floral centerpieces for the tables.

Laughter filled the museum as everyone pitched in to make the workload much lighter.

Amy was setting out place cards when Miles came up from behind and wrapped his arms around her.

"Take a second and look around, Amy," he said. "All the people we love most in the world are in one building, just for us."

Amy smiled, loving Miles's arms around her.

"And tomorrow, we'll all officially become one family," he said. He kissed her cheek. "I can't remember ever being happier."

Amy put her hand on his cheek, feeling joyful tears pricking her eyes. The girls were helping Sara and Robin with the centerpieces while Matt, Colton, and Kai put chair covers on the chairs with Miles's brothers. Mimi and Tracy chatted as they decorated the cake table, and Miles's sisters-in-law set up the snack table.

Miles gently turned Amy until she faced him.

"Thank you," he said.

"For what?" she whispered.

"For saying yes to me."

"Thank you for asking."

He grinned as he hugged her tight. They were soon chastised by Miles's dad, who told them to save all the hugging and kissing for tomorrow. Amy laughed, gave Miles one more kiss, and then went back to setting out the place cards while Clarence pulled Miles away to hang white lights from the ceiling.

Time sped by, and they were soon done decorating, but Amy could hardly enjoy their efforts because they had to be at the church for the rehearsal. More extended family arrived, including Kevin with Aiden and Zoe, and Chad and Anna with Corbin, Emerson, and baby Elizabeth Pearl.

The rehearsal went well, since the wedding party was small. Amy and Tracy's parents had died in a car accident when Amy was in college, so she had opted to ask Matt and Jana to walk her down the aisle. Miles would come out at the front of the church with Natalie and Colton at his side, and then the girls would stand with Amy and the boys would stand with Miles. Robin and Tracy were Amy's bridesmaids, and Miles's brothers were his groomsmen.

Soon, they were done with the rehearsal and off to the hotel where Mimi and Clarence had rented a large room and had the rehearsal dinner catered by Amore. There was pasta with both marina or white sauce, a large Caesar salad, breadsticks, and gelato and tiramisu for dessert. Italian sodas and coffee were also served, and Amy made a concentrated effort to relax and enjoy family time.

Everything went as expected, though the snowstorm picked up in intensity. Amy started to get calls and texts from people who weren't sure if they could make it to the wedding the next day. With each message, her heart sank a little more, though she tried to rally, knowing that the most important people in her life were already there.

When the meal came to an end, Amy stood up to start cleaning, but Mimi put her hands on Amy's shoulders and nudged her to the door. "Go. Spend a little quiet time with Miles before everyone needs to head home to bed. We've got this under control. It's one of our gifts to you."

Miles had heard, so he took Amy's hand. "Thanks, Mom."

He led her out of the room and toward the quiet lobby where two oversized chairs faced a large gas fireplace. He gestured to one of the chairs, and she took a seat while he sat on the other one. They were close enough to keep holding hands.

She stifled a yawn, which made him yawn—causing both of them to laugh.

"I'm looking forward to our getaway to Quincy," Amy said after she removed her hand from her mouth. "But I'm afraid I might sleep the whole time we're there."

Miles grinned. "We've accomplished a lot these past few weeks. I'm ready to relax a little bit and enjoy being married and living in the same house."

"Me too."

They spoke of the day, chatted about some of the things that one or the other needed to remember for tomorrow, and simply enjoyed each other's company in the stillness.

Outside, the snow continued to fall, piling up near the large windows.

"I'm sorry about the snow," Miles said.

"I am too," she said. "But if I've learned anything over the past few weeks, it's that everything happens for a reason. Whether someone tries to sabotage our wedding and we end up getting a better caterer and a better reception hall, or my family's wedding veil goes missing and we find it in the museum where it was forgotten, or the kids fight and it leads us to have an important conversation that might not have come up otherwise, these things are not coincidental. God has His hand in our lives in big ways and small ways, always pointing us toward Him and toward each other. The longer and harder we fight, the more difficult it is to learn our lessons."

"I like that," Miles said. "And you're right. God doesn't allow anything to go wasted. In His economy, even the smallest issue can be used for our good and His glory."

Amy nodded, feeling lighter and freer than she had in weeks.

"Tomorrow is going to be a good day, Miles, no matter how much it snows or how many things go wrong. Because we are getting married and becoming a family. That's the most important thing that could ever happen to us."

And she could hardly wait.

Everything was cleaned up, Matt and Jana waited in the car, and Amy was freezing as she stood outside her vehicle to say good night to Miles. The snow hit her skin and melted. It gathered on her head and shoulders and covered her car—and it didn't look like it was going to let up anytime soon.

"Good night," Miles said, coming alongside her. Natalie and Colton were in his Jeep, waiting to head home.

"Tonight is the last night we will ever need to be apart," Amy said as she wiped the snow off his shoulders.

Miles grinned. "I love you, Amy."

"I love you too, Miles. I'll see you at the church tomorrow afternoon."

"It feels like that's a lifetime to wait."

"Just a blink of an eye compared to the time we've already waited." She smiled and stood on tiptoe to offer him a kiss.

"I'll drop Natalie off at nine and pick up Matt," he said as he pulled back.

"I can't wait."

They hugged once more, and then Amy got into her car and left the hotel parking lot, turning in the opposite direction as Miles.

She drove slowly, since the roads hadn't been plowed yet, but she still slid past a stop sign and couldn't see the center line of the road. Matt and Jana were quiet in the back seat, and when she glanced in the rearview mirror, she saw both yawning and their heads dipping as they tried to stay awake.

Finally, they arrived at Tracy's. Despite the late hour, several lights were on in the house.

"I want both of you to take a quick shower and then it's off to bed," Amy said to her kids as they got out of the car. "And be careful on the snow. I don't want you falling and getting hurt."

The kids did as she instructed, though the snow seemed to revive Matt, who stopped to make a snowball and throw it at his sister. Jana ran screaming toward the house and slipped once but righted herself before she fell.

"Matt," Amy said in a stern voice.

He smiled sheepishly and then went into the house.

Amy paused for a second in the soft, quiet stillness of the night and said a prayer of thanksgiving for the blessings in her life. She had a feeling the following day would be busy and a little chaotic and wanted to take the time to just soak up the wonder of it all.

But it was cold, so she didn't take long. Her arms were full of things she would need in the morning to get ready for the wedding.

"There you are," Tracy said as she met Amy in the entryway. "I already sent the kids upstairs to take their showers."

"Thank you. Here, can you take this?" Amy handed a bag to Tracy and then slipped off her shoes and removed her coat.

"I love how the museum turned out," Tracy said. "It's going to be so pretty tomorrow. Do you like it?"

"I do. It's better than I had imagined," Amy said.

"Let's just pray that the snow stops soon and the plows get out before tomorrow afternoon." Tracy handed Amy back her bag. "I have something I want to give you before you go to bed. Do you have a minute?"

"Of course. I'm so ready for this wedding, I don't think there's much left to do tonight."

"Good. What I want to give you is in here."

Amy followed Tracy into the living room. The fireplace crackled, offering a soft, comfortable warmth.

"Jeff already went to bed," Tracy said as she crossed to the bookshelf next to the fireplace. "He was up early today for work." She nodded at the couch. "Have a seat."

Amy sat and set her bag next to her feet. She knew she needed to get to bed too, but she wasn't sure how well she would sleep. She was both nervous and excited for tomorrow—a combination that might make it hard to relax.

Tracy removed a black book from the shelf and brought it to Amy. "I have a gift for you."

"A gift?" Amy frowned. "You've already done so much, Tracy."

"It's not from me," Tracy said with a smile.

"Not from you?" Amy tilted her head, confused by Tracy's tears.

Tracy sat next to Amy and handed her the book. It was a leather Bible with gold lettering and beautiful scrollwork.

"Who is this from?" Amy asked.

"Open it." Tracy sat back and watched Amy with more tears coming to her eyes.

Frowning deeper, Amy opened the front cover of the Bible, and her breath caught.

It was from Grandma Pearl.

"She bought each of her grandchildren a Bible for a wedding gift," Tracy said. "Both Robin and I have one very similar to it."

"Oh, Tracy," Amy said as tears burned her eyes.

"When Grandma knew she was dying," Tracy continued, "she reminded me of the Bible and asked if I would give it to you the night before your wedding. I've been keeping it for you ever since."

"Grandma," Amy whispered as she ran her finger over the inscription. "'To Amy, love Grandma Pearl.'"

"There's something else inside," Tracy said.

Amy flipped a few pages and found a note-sized envelope tucked in the Book of Genesis. Amy's name was written on the front of the envelope in Grandma's familiar handwriting.

Tracy stood and put her hand on Amy's shoulder. "Right before my wedding, Grandma Pearl sat me down and gave me her wisdom and advice about marriage." She smiled. "I'll never forget her words. Before she died, she told me that she had written you a note, telling you what she would want you to know if she could be here herself." Tracy kissed the top of Amy's head. "Goodnight, Amy. I'll leave you and Grandma alone, and I'll see you bright and early tomorrow morning."

Amy reached out and took Tracy's hand, tears slipping down her cheeks. "Thank you, Tracy, for everything."

Tracy smiled and put her hand over Amy's for a moment before she left the living room and went upstairs.

Amy sat for a few seconds, looking at the envelope, thanking Grandma Pearl for her thoughtfulness. Though she wasn't alive anymore, Grandma Pearl had found a way to be present.

Slowly, Amy opened the envelope and pulled out a piece of stationery with delicate bluebells around the edges, reminding Amy of the handkerchief she was borrowing for the wedding from Tracy.

The tears made it hard to read the spidery handwriting, but Amy instantly felt like she was sitting with Grandma Pearl in her living room, the warm, sweet voice filling her with love and hope.

> *My Dearest Amy,*
>
> *If you're reading this, then you are about to embark upon one of life's greatest, and often most perilous, journeys—and I am not there with you. I wish I could meet your husband and watch you take this big step, but it gives me joy to know that whoever you choose, I already love him. You are a wise and kindhearted woman, and you will choose an equally wise and kindhearted man. I don't need to meet him to know that he is perfect for you.*
>
> *Marriage is a gift from God Almighty, one that will change you in ways you can't even imagine right now. Loving your husband will be easy. Liking him on some days will be hard. It will be both wonderful and difficult, depending on the day, the week, or the month. Good marriages are full of forgiveness, trust, and hard work. Great marriages are built, year by year, by overcoming adversity together. And you will have adversity, my darling girl. I would wish you a life*

without trouble, but it's in the trouble that we learn our most important lessons.

I wish I could teach you what I learned while married to your grandpa Howard, but those are things you and your husband will have to discover together. And the discovery is the best part! The lessons you'll learn in your marriage cannot be taught. They must be experienced. And as you experience difficulties, you will learn how to rely on each other and on God, growing stronger with each passing year. My only advice for you is summed up perfectly in 1 Corinthians 13. Be patient, be kind. Do not be envious or boastful or proud. Do not dishonor your husband or seek only what is best for you. Do not become easily angered toward one another, and do not keep records of his wrongdoings. That only leads to bitterness and resentment. Remember that your love for each other should not delight in anything evil but always rejoice with the truth. Protect each other, trust each other, dream and hope together, and your love will persevere.

I pray that you have many, many happy years together. They won't be perfect, but they will stack, one upon the other, to create your unique and beautiful love story. The good and the bad, the hard and the easy, the extraordinary and the mundane. Do not let anyone else tell you how to write your story, Amy. That's for you and your husband to decide.

My gift to you is this Bible. You'll see that there is space for your wedding date as well as for the births and baptisms of your children. May you and your husband and your children love the Lord all the days He gives you on this earth.

I will close by speaking a prayer over your marriage. It is my hope that you'll hold these words close and, when you think of them, you'll know that I'm there with you, loving you with all my heart.

May God bless and keep you both, may God's face shine on you. May He be kind to you and give you peace.

I love you,

Grandma Pearl

Amy folded the note and pressed it to her lips as more tears fell. She would share the letter with Miles and reread it whenever she needed to feel close to Grandma Pearl.

With a deep breath, Amy rose from the couch and headed toward the stairs with the Bible and the note in hand.

Tomorrow was her wedding day, and she was ready.

Chapter Nineteen

*A*my had thought she'd be nervous for her wedding, but she'd never felt calmer or more certain of anything in her life. Marrying Miles felt as natural as breathing. Joining their families together was the icing on the cake.

"You look beautiful, Amy," Tracy said as she stood back and admired Amy in the bride's room at the church thirty minutes before the ceremony. "I've never seen anyone glow like you're glowing today."

Amy glanced in the mirror and couldn't deny what Tracy said. Her cheeks were tinged with pink, and her eyes had a sparkle to them that nothing could diminish. She was happy. Truly happy.

"There's only one more thing," Robin said. She walked across the room to get the veil, which was draped over a wooden hanger.

The space they had commandeered for the bride's room was usually a children's Sunday school classroom, so Jana and Natalie sat on low chairs, looking up at Amy as she got ready. They wore identical pink dresses, which they had helped to pick out, and matching pink shoes. Robin and Tracy had spent an hour curling their hair and styling it with little pearls that matched the pearls in Amy's updo. The girls had giggled and loved all the glamourous attention. They'd even been allowed to put a little rouge on their cheeks and a hint of pink gloss on their lips.

"It's days like today that I miss Mom and Dad the most," Amy said as she continued to look at her reflection in the mirror. "And Grandma Pearl. More than anything, I wish they could be here with us."

"Me too," Tracy agreed as she pushed a bobby pin back into Amy's hair. "But they're here with us in a way. Even when we lose someone, we don't lose their love."

"I know." Amy turned away from the mirror to look at the clock. Two thirty. Amy hadn't seen Miles all day and didn't plan to see him until the ceremony started. They would take pictures afterward as their guests made their way to the museum, and then the wedding party would join them there for supper. The day had sped by, but at that moment it felt like time crawled. She couldn't wait to see Miles.

"Ready for the veil?" Robin asked.

Amy nodded. It was the last thing she needed and then she'd be ready to walk down the aisle.

Sara stood by with her camera. She'd been taking pictures throughout the day as they'd gotten ready at Tracy's house and then headed to the church. Sara had left Amy for about thirty minutes to take pictures of the guys as they got ready in the groom's room. The professional photographer was setting up in the sanctuary. Amy wanted to see the pictures Sara had taken, but she refrained from asking Sara because she wanted the moment she saw Miles to be special.

Amy looked back into the mirror as Robin and Tracy placed the wedding veil on her head.

Tears came to all their eyes as they arranged the headpiece and laid the folds of the sheer fabric around Amy's shoulders. She'd never felt closer to the women in her family. There was something special in knowing that she was the seventh bride to wear the cherished veil on her wedding day.

It was a chapel-length veil that draped to the floor. Amy would need to be careful not to step on it or tear it. She would remove it after their pictures were taken, and Tracy would put it back in the acid-free storage box, to be tucked away in Grandma's attic for the next family wedding.

But, for now, it was Amy's.

"I didn't think you could look any prettier," Natalie a sigh. "But you do."

Amy turned and smiled at her soon-to-be daughter. "Thank you, Natalie."

"Can I get a picture with you and the girls?" Sara asked.

Nodding, Amy gathered the girls to her side.

"Now the bridesmaids," Sara said as she indicated for Tracy and Robin to join the group.

"We have a little time," Sara said after a few shots. "Why don't we see if the groomsmen and ring bearers are ready so I can get a few pictures of all of you together. It might be fun to have some more casual pictures besides the formal ones that will be taken after the ceremony."

"Do you mind if we leave you?" Tracy asked Amy.

Amy shook her head. "I wouldn't mind a little time alone, actually."

"Perfect." Sara put her hands on the girls' shoulders. "We'll be back in about twenty minutes to line up for the procession. Come on, girls."

The wedding party filed out of the bride's room, leaving Amy alone for the first time since that morning when she'd woken up in the guest room at Tracy's house.

She took a deep breath and walked to the window to look out at the snow-covered landscape. Thankfully, the storm had passed early that morning and the plows had come out to clean up the streets. From Amy's vantage point, she could see part of the parking lot, and it looked full. She was thankful that so many people had been able to come.

The door opened, and Amy turned, expecting to see one of the wedding party. But it was Stephanie who stood on the threshold.

Amy's lips parted in surprise. Stephanie was the last person she expected to see today.

"What are you doing here?" Amy asked, her surprise turning to worry.

Stephanie looked at Amy, her gaze slicing from the top of her veiled head to the hem of her lacy skirt.

"I think the better question is, what are you doing here, Amy?"

Amy stared at Stephanie, confused by her strange question.

"I'm marrying Miles," Amy said. "Why would you ask me that?"

Stephanie stepped into the room. "I tried to warn you, even before I came to Canton, that you shouldn't let this wedding proceed. But you didn't listen to me."

"That's because Miles and I are in love and we are getting married today!" Amy took a step toward Stephanie, anger replacing her other emotions. "You need to leave, Stephanie. You were not invited to be here today, and I can't think of any reason you should have come."

"I came to stop this wedding. If you won't put a stop to it, then I'll go to Miles, and he'll put a stop to it."

"No." Amy was suddenly afraid that Stephanie was mentally unstable. "He won't. You need to leave."

"Not until I can talk some sense into you or Miles." She took a deep breath, and tears came to her eyes. "Miles is supposed to be with me. That's why I came back to Canton. I'm in love with him. I was going to show him that he made a mistake when he stopped dating me. It's why I left travel nursing and went back to school to become a nurse practitioner. I wanted to join him, wherever he was, and work beside him. If that meant here, in Canton, then that's what I planned to do for the rest of my life. I didn't know that he was engaged or that I was buying his fiancée's house." She took a step closer to Amy. "You're the one who messed everything up. If it hadn't been for you, I would be rekindling my romance with Miles right now."

"You don't know that that's true," Amy said, her senses going on alert. She didn't want to make Stephanie angry. She was unsure if she was dangerous.

"And we'll never know," Stephanie said, "unless you step aside and let Miles love me."

Amy took a deep breath, praying for wisdom. "I won't do that, Stephanie. I'm marrying Miles today. You need to accept that and move on."

Stephanie shook her head. "I don't want to accept that."

"You have no choice. You can't force someone to love you. I'm sorry. Perhaps there will be someone else down the road for you to love. But it won't be Miles."

Stephanie lifted her chin. "I don't want anyone but Miles. And I won't leave until you call off this wedding or I can talk him into calling it off. I won't take no for an answer."

"I won't call off my wedding," Amy said, incredulous. The nerve of her! "And neither will Miles."

"We'll see about that." Stephanie turned to leave the room, but someone stepped into her path, stopping her.

It was Miles.

He stood in the hall, but his gaze slipped to Amy, and a look of wonder came over his face.

"Amy," he said, his voice just above a whisper, "you're breathtaking."

Amy's heart sped up as warmth filled her at the sight of her groom.

Stephanie stood between them, facing Miles, but he didn't even seem aware of her.

"I was just coming to find you," she said.

Miles tore his gaze away from Amy, and a look of disgust settled on his face. "This is the last time you will try to interfere in my life, Stephanie. I've told you repeatedly that you are not welcome or wanted here. I don't know what else to say."

"Please, Miles." Stephanie tried to reach for him, but he stepped away.

"I'm calling the police, Stephanie, and I will be petitioning the courts for a restraining order."

Stephanie took a step back. "A restraining order?"

"Yes. I don't want you anywhere near my family. Do you understand?" The look on his face was fierce. Amy had never seen anything like it. Miles was protecting his family, and Amy loved him all the more for it.

"You're serious," Stephanie said.

"I've never been more serious in my life. You are not allowed to speak to Amy ever again, do you understand? And I don't want you near our children either. As far as I'm concerned, you are a stranger to us, and that's how I want it to remain."

Amy couldn't see Stephanie's face, but she could see the rigid outline of her body as her chin slowly came up in defiance. "This has been a waste of my time."

"It certainly has," Miles agreed.

"Fine," Stephanie said. "I'm resigning on Monday, and I'll be leaving Canton for good. I didn't want to live in this little dirt town anyway. I only came for you."

Miles pointed down the hall. "The exit is that way."

Stephanie huffed and stormed out of the room. Amy heard a door slam a moment later.

Miles turned his gaze back to Amy, but the look he gave her was hard to read. It was sad and full of disappointment yet mingled with love and admiration.

"I'm sorry, Amy," he said as he remained just outside the room. "I know we said we wouldn't see each other until the ceremony started. But when I heard Stephanie's voice coming from this way, I knew I couldn't—" He paused as a smile tilted his lips. "What?"

Amy was smiling at him. "I don't mind," she said. She walked across the room to join him. "I wish she hadn't come and ruined this moment for us, but it seems so appropriate now. Nothing has gone as we planned, has it?" She laughed and shook her head, slowly growing more serious, thankful that Stephanie was gone for good. "But now we get this moment alone together, before we have to stand in front of hundreds of people, and we can enjoy our first glimpse of each other without anyone watching us."

He stepped over the threshold and into the room, his face softening. "You're right." He cradled Amy's cheek in his hand, love and affection gleaming in his gaze. "You are stunning, Amy, more beautiful today than you were when I first fell in love with you over thirty years ago. And I know that you will only get lovelier as the years go by."

Amy put her hand over his. "You look stunning too." He wore a black suit and tie with a pink rosebud corsage.

He lowered his hand. "As much as I want to kiss you, I'll save that for the wedding." He winked at her. "I should probably get back to the groom's end of the hallway before someone finds us."

Amy grinned. "I'll see you soon."

"Not soon enough."

And with that, Miles left.

But Amy wasn't sad. In less than an hour, she'd be his wife.

"Are you nervous, Mom?" Matt asked fifteen minutes later as they stood in the church lobby, waiting to enter the sanctuary. Matt stood to Amy's right, and Jana stood to her left. They both looked up at her.

"No," Amy said with a smile at Matt. "I'm not nervous. I'm just excited. Are you nervous?"

Matt shook his head. "I'm excited too. It's been a long time since I had a dad."

Amy gave Matt a hug, holding him close. "I love you, buddy."

"I love you too," Matt said. Then he pulled back, readjusted his suit, and smoothed his hair. "But don't do that again, please. It took me a long time to look this good."

Amy tried to hide her laughter, but Tracy must have heard, because she turned around and grinned.

"What about you?" Amy asked Jana. "Are you nervous?"

Jana shook her head. "Nope. Not me. I know exactly what I'm doing."

"Good."

"We're about ready," Miles's sister-in-law said from her place near the sanctuary doors. She held a cell phone. Her husband must have just texted her to let her know that Miles and his groomsmen, along with Colton and Natalie, were entering the sanctuary at the front of the church.

Amy nodded at her soon-to-be sister-in-law that she was ready.

Everyone turned to look toward the back of the church as Robin entered. Amy had a clear view of the sanctuary and was happy to see so many familiar faces.

After Robin, Tracy went next, and then it was Amy's turn with Matt and Jana.

Matt offered Amy his elbow, so Amy slipped her right hand through and linked elbows with him. She shifted her bouquet to her right hand and then took Jana's hand in her left one.

The organist started playing "The Bridal Chorus," and everyone stood and turned to watch Amy and the kids walk down the aisle.

She smiled as tears formed in her eyes. So many people looked back at her, truly happy to celebrate this day. Friends and coworkers, including Tawny, and Amy's boss and friend, Kelly Walker, plus people from her old job in Steelville. Family had also come from near and far, including Aunt Abigail and so many others. Miles's parents were seated in the front row, next to Miles's sisters-in-law.

But everything and everyone else faded as soon as Amy caught Miles's gaze from the front of the church. Natalie held his hand while Colton stood next to him, and both smiled at Amy. She smiled back and then looked at Miles again.

All thoughts of Stephanie, of Beverly's attempt to sabotage the wedding, and of the missing veil slipped from her mind. All she could think about was Miles and how happy she was to become his wife. If she could have, she would have run down the aisle.

When she finally arrived at the front of the church, Pastor Gary said, "Who gives this woman to be married?"

"We do," Matt and Jana said, though Jana added a little giggle.

"And who gives this man to be married?" he asked.

"We do," Colton and Natalie said.

Amy and Miles hugged each of the children before he took her hand in his and the kids found their places, just like they had practiced.

Tracy and Robin wiped tears from their eyes as Amy handed her bouquet to Tracy to hold during the ceremony.

"You may be seated," Pastor Gary told the congregation.

Amy stood next to Miles, her hand in his, and she realized, from this moment on, they would be together as husband and wife. This was the moment when their lives were truly blending, when there would no longer be her kids and Miles's kids, but their kids. When they would no longer be Miles Anderson and Amy Allen, but Miles and Amy Anderson. More than that, in the eyes of God, the two were becoming one. Amy stood in awe of marriage, and though she knew millions of people before her had been married, the newness and mystery of it felt unique to her and Miles.

Soon it was time to share their vows and exchange the rings.

"Miles," Pastor Gary said, "please repeat after me."

Miles repeated the familiar words. "I, Miles Clarence Anderson, take you, Amy Vivian Allen, to be my wife." He placed the wedding band on her finger. "I promise to be faithful to you in good times and in bad, in sickness and in health, to love you and to honor you all the days of my life."

When it was time for Amy to repeat the words, she spoke them with such conviction, tears fell from her eyes as she put the wedding band on Miles's finger.

"I, Amy Vivian Allen, take you, Miles Clarence Anderson, to be my husband. I promise to be faithful to you in good times and in bad, in sickness and in health, to love you and to honor you all the days of my life."

"Miles and Amy," Pastor Gary said, "since you have consented together in holy matrimony, and have pledged yourselves to each other by your solemn vows and by the giving and receiving of rings, and have declared your commitment before God and these witnesses, I now pronounce you husband and wife in the name of the Father and of the Son and of the Holy Spirit. Those whom God has joined together, let no one separate. Miles, you may kiss your bride."

Miles took Amy into his arms and gave her a kiss that put all their other kisses to shame.

With warm cheeks and an applause that filled the church, Amy and Miles turned to their friends and family as husband and wife.

Finally.

✦ Chapter Twenty ✦

*A*my couldn't stop smiling as she walked up the aisle with Miles, as they greeted their guests in the receiving line, as they took pictures in the sanctuary, and, finally, as they stepped into Miles's Jeep to head to the reception. It was impossible to wipe the grin off her face.

"My cheeks hurt," she said as she rubbed them gently. "I can't remember ever being this happy."

"So do mine." Miles leaned over from the driver's seat and kissed her again—this time without an audience. "I love you, Amy Anderson."

"I love you too," she whispered, feeling like a giddy young bride.

The kids had gone to the reception with Tracy and Jeff, leaving Miles and Amy alone for a few minutes to revel in the newness of their marriage.

"I can hardly believe we're finally married," Amy said. "Who could have ever imagined the course our love story would take?"

Miles shook his head. "We've missed a lot of life together, but I know we'll make up in quality what other people have in quantity. I know how precious marriage is and how fragile it can be if it's not tended to properly. I promise I will always put our marriage first, Amy, and I will protect it with everything I possess."

Amy nodded. "I will too."

He glanced at the almost-empty parking lot. "I kind of want to just skip the reception and run away with you."

Amy laughed. "I think there would be a lot of unhappy people if we did that—especially our children."

"Yeah." He turned on the car, chuckling. "I suppose you're right."

They drove to the museum and were greeted by dozens of friends and family at the door with noisemakers and bubbles.

"Amy!" Tracy said when she found them in the chaos. "Congratulations!"

Amy hugged Tracy tight. They hadn't had much opportunity to talk since the ceremony ended. "Thank you for everything."

"You're welcome. I'm so happy for you and Miles and the kids."

"Me too," Amy said. "And you don't mind having them for a couple of nights?"

"Of course not." Tracy smiled. "I love having them at our house."

After the reception, the kids would go home with Tracy and Jeff, and Amy and Miles would drive the twenty minutes to Quincy and stay in a hotel for a couple of nights to have a little time to themselves.

There were other people waiting for Amy's attention, so Tracy told her they'd talk later.

Miles stood near Amy as if he didn't want to be separated from her. She didn't want to leave his side either. Soon enough, they'd have to go back to work and their wedding day would become a memory. Until then, she wanted to make it last as long as possible.

The museum looked enchanting with the twinkle lights strung across the room, offering a gentle glow on the dozens of tables below.

Each table was covered in a white cloth, with a soft pink runner down the middle. Fresh flower bouquets encircled by tea lights sat in the center. White chair covers made everything look elegant and clean. The exhibits around the room added a unique, exotic flavor to the delicacy of the flowers and lighting.

"Mama!" Jana said as she ran up to Amy.

Amy bent down and received Jana's hug and saw that Natalie wasn't far behind—which didn't surprise Amy.

Natalie was just as exuberant as Jana. "We're married!"

Miles grinned as Matt and Colton sauntered up, punch glasses in hand.

"We're not married," Colton said with a wrinkle of his nose at his sister. "They're married."

"Yes, we are," Natalie said. "We're all a family, so we're all married."

"Dad?" Colton said with annoyance in his voice, as if to say, can you please talk some sense into her?

"What Natalie means," Miles said, as he entwined his fingers through Amy's, "is that when Amy and I got married, we married our families together, so we're all now one big family."

"We're married!" Natalie said again, jumping up and down in her excitement.

Miles shrugged at Colton. "I guess we're all married."

"Natalie is going to call Mom, Mom," Jana said to Miles, acting a little bashful as she swung her shoulders back and forth. "Can I call you Daddy, like Natalie does?"

Miles knelt and took Jana's hands. "Nothing would make me happier, Jana. Being your dad is one of the greatest privileges of my life and always will be." He looked at Matt, who watched in silence. "And your dad too, Matt, if you'll let me."

Matt grinned and nodded.

Amy looked at Colton, who would be the hardest one to read. Did he want to call her Mom, like the other kids? Or would he feel more comfortable calling her Amy?

Colton glanced at Amy, as if he knew what she was thinking.

Miles stood straight again and gave Amy an encouraging smile.

"Colton," Amy said, "you don't need to call me Mom, but I want you to know that I would be honored if you did. Whether you call me Mom or not, you are just as much my son as Matt is."

Colton shrugged in a non-committal way—and Amy was okay with that. Some things would need time. She was just thankful he hadn't said an outright no.

Slowly, Amy and Miles were able to work through the crowd to get to the head table. Supper was served at six o'clock, and it was as delicious as Amy had hoped.

"Look at that," Amy said as she and Miles ate their meal with the wedding party. "I love seeing how happy everyone is today."

Miles glanced up and took in the room, full of their loved ones. "Weddings really are one of the happiest celebrations, aren't they?"

"It's because of hope," Amy said without hesitation. "Weddings fill people with hope for the future and hope in the love that two people share. That love makes people believe in the goodness of humanity. And I think all of us need that reminder from time to time."

When the meal was finished, Miles and Amy stood to cut the cake. It was beautiful, proving that Trish was the right person for the job.

Everyone clapped as Miles and Amy took up the cake knife and sliced into the moist center within. The photographer took more pictures as they fed each other a piece of cake and their guests clapped.

When they were done, they returned to the head table where Tracy and Miles's brother prepared to give their maid of honor and best man speeches.

First, it was Tracy's turn. She took up the microphone, and before she even began to talk, she had tears in her eyes.

The room quieted as Tracy smiled at Amy and then at Miles.

"For those who don't know me," Tracy began, "I'm Tracy Doyle, Amy's older sister. I'm here today, not only as the maid of honor, but also as our family representative. Sadly, our parents passed away twenty-six years ago, but I know they are here with us today in our hearts and they would be over the moon to welcome Miles, Colton, and Natalie into our family. Almost as happy as I am." She smiled again, and Amy could see she was trying to control her emotions. "Life is full of difficulty, so in moments like this, as we come together to celebrate something beautiful and good, it's important to take a minute to just soak up the joy around us. As I look at this room, full of the wonderful people that make up Amy and Miles's life, there is so much love to be had. Thank you all for being with us today as we celebrate this amazing love story."

Miles took Amy's hand, squeezing it gently.

"Amy and Miles met in elementary school and were friends for years," Tracy continued. "In high school, they began to date, and even then, I knew they were meant for one another. They fit so well, so effortlessly. Unfortunately, college pulled them apart and kept them apart for over thirty years. But, in those years apart, they only became more perfect for each other. As they journeyed through life, each on their own path, they gathered valuable lessons, experiences, and gifts that they've brought to their marriage today. The four most important are Matt, Jana, Colton, and Natalie." Tracy smiled at the kids, who still sat at the head table. "And though their paths weren't perfect or without trouble, they were slowly wending toward one another and crossed at just the right time."

Amy wiped tears from her eyes.

"Today, we've all been invited to witness the beginning of a new family, and what an honor it is to see. I invite all of you to join me in continuing to pray for Amy and Miles and their children that God would bless them abundantly and that they would bless those around them." She turned back to Amy and Miles. "Congratulations, you two. I'm so happy for you."

Everyone clapped, and Tracy raised her glass to them and then sat down to allow the best man to give his speech.

As Amy listened to her new brother-in-law, her heart was so full, she had to place her hand against her chest to contain her joy.

Her wedding had been perfect—and it proved to her that despite disappointments, setbacks, and obstacles, it was still possible to have everything her heart desired.

It was a great reminder that her marriage would be the same.

"Mom and Daddy are here!" Natalie yelled into Tracy's house from the front door on Monday evening. "They're here, they're here!"

Miles smiled at Amy and squeezed her hand. Gentle snowflakes fell from the dark sky as they walked up to the porch. They'd had two glorious days of sleeping in, going out to eat, sitting in the hot tub, and uninterrupted conversations. No work, no worries, and nothing to do but enjoy each other's company.

Amy had never cherished two days more in her entire life.

Tomorrow, they would go back to work, and soon dishes, laundry, and parenting would rush in and remind them that their short honeymoon was over. But it was just the beginning of their happily-ever-after.

"We need to make sure we set aside time to get away together as often as possible," Miles said as the other children appeared at the front door, just as eager to see Miles and Amy as Natalie had been. Scrappy was with Robin and Terry, and they wouldn't go get him until tomorrow after school.

"That sounds wonderful," Amy said. "I'm already looking forward to the next getaway."

"Hey," Tracy said as she joined the children, "I know you're all anxious to get home. Everyone's bags are packed, and they're ready to go."

"I can't wait!" Jana called. "I get the top bunk tonight."

Amy grinned. She was just as eager as Jana to settle into their house and start finding their new normal. It had been over a week since they'd moved out of their old house, and being in limbo at Tracy's wasn't ideal. Especially when Matt and Jana had made so many adjustments and moves in their short lives.

Jana and Natalie threw their arms around Amy, and then they ran to get their coats. Matt was next in line to get a hug from Amy, and then he surprised them both and hugged Miles.

"I missed you, Dad," Matt said. He looked up at Miles and smiled.

Tenderness filled Miles's face as he returned Matt's hug. "I missed you too, buddy."

Colton was the only one who held back, watching the interaction with uncertainty.

Amy put her hand on his shoulder. "We missed all of you," she said. "You guys were all that we could talk about while we were away."

Colton didn't reach out to Amy, but he didn't pull away either, and she considered that a win.

"Everyone's homework is done," Tracy said, helping the kids grab their backpacks and their bags. Colton and Natalie had brought overnight bags, but Matt and Jana had their suitcases. "We had a big supper, so I don't think they'll be hungry, but boy, can those boys eat."

"They'll probably eat us out of house and home," Miles said, ruffling Colton's hair. "This one would eat an entire box of cereal in one sitting if I let him."

"I'm a growing boy," Colton said, grinning.

"Thank you so much, Tracy," Amy said as she gave her sister a hug. "We owe you and Jeff a debt of gratitude."

"We're happy to help," she said. Jeff joined their little group and put his arm around Tracy.

"We'll take you out for supper soon," Miles promised. "You just name the date."

"I'll call you," Tracy said to Amy.

"Perfect." Amy smiled, eager to be on their way home. "See you guys later."

Everyone called out their goodbyes as they left Jeff and Tracy's house and headed to the two vehicles.

"Now that the wedding is behind us," Miles said, "we need to look at getting you a minivan or an SUV. Something that fits all six of us."

Amy nodded as she helped Jana with her suitcase. When the group parted at the end of the sidewalk, Amy and the girls to one vehicle and Miles and the boys to the other, Amy said, "We'll see you at home."

Miles grinned and winked at her. "See you there."

It only took a few minutes to drive from Tracy's house back home, but the girls shared almost every detail of their two nights apart. They were so animated and excited, Amy was afraid they wouldn't be able to calm down to go to bed.

Amy was the first to pull into the driveway, with Miles close behind. Light shone from Beverly's house next door, illuminating her beautiful stained-glass window. Though it was a reminder of all that Beverly had put them through, Amy realized that she held no ill will toward her new neighbor. Somehow, they would find a way to befriend her.

The kids were loud and energetic as Amy tugged Jana's suitcase out of the car and walked up to the back door. She pulled out her housekey, put it into the lock, and pushed open the door. The girls ran inside.

Colton and Matt barreled into the house next, and Amy had to call out to Matt to remind him to unpack his suitcase.

"Will do, Mom," he called back.

Amy set her keys on the counter and put down Jana's suitcase. It was too big for the little girl to haul up the steps on her own, so Amy would have to take it up for her.

Miles entered next, carrying his and Amy's suitcase from their trip. He closed the door and set the suitcase on the kitchen table and then suddenly turned to Amy.

"I forgot to carry you over the threshold!"

Amy frowned. "Miles—"

"Come here," he said with a grin.

"Don't you dare!" she protested as she moved away from him, laughing. "You'll hurt yourself."

He caught her and wrapped her in his arms, laughter in his voice. "It's bad luck to not carry you over the threshold."

"Ha," Amy said. She returned his hug, loving the feel of his arms around her. "I don't believe in bad luck. Besides, you and I have done nothing like we were supposed to, yet it's been perfect. I say we don't stop now."

Miles leaned his forehead against hers. "That's a deal, Mrs. Anderson."

Amy laid her head against his chest and closed her eyes, savoring the moment, wishing she could hold on to it forever.

"What do you say we lock up the house, get those kids to bed, and then fall asleep watching a movie together. And, this time, you can stay the night."

"That's a deal, Dr. Anderson," Amy said. "And then I'll stay the next night, and the next, and the next."

"Promise?" Miles asked.

"I do."

And she would keep saying I do for the rest of her life.

Dear Reader,

What a joy it was to write Amy and Miles's wedding story! I had the privilege of introducing Miles, Colton, and Natalie in this series back in book four. It was so much fun to envision their two families finally joining together. I hope you enjoyed this addition to the Secrets from Grandma's Attic series as much as I did.

As I thought about Amy's wedding, I tried to imagine what she might look for in Grandma's attic to celebrate her happy occasion, and I thought of a wedding veil. In my own life, I also went looking for a veil when I planned my wedding. My mom and dad were married in 1974, and my mom sold her dress and veil in a garage sale for twenty-five dollars soon after. I always wished she had kept them. I asked her who she sold them to, and I found the name and number in our local phone book. When I called the new owner, I was delighted to hear that she had decided to elope and hadn't worn either of them! They had hung in her closet for twenty-seven years, unused. I asked her if she'd sell them back to me, and she said she would—for twenty-five dollars!

Unfortunately, the dress was a little outdated and the veil was torn and stained, so I wasn't able to use them. But I still love knowing that our family owns my mother's wedding dress again, and if my daughters, nieces, or granddaughters choose to use it, I will have it for them. There's something special about a family wedding dress or veil to pass down through the generations.

Thank you for returning with us to Grandma's attic!

Signed,
Gabrielle

About The Author

Gabrielle Meyer lives in central Minnesota on the banks of the upper Mississippi River with her husband and four children. As an employee of the Minnesota Historical Society, she fell in love with the rich history of her state and enjoys writing fictional stories inspired by real people, places, and events.

COLLECTIBLES *From* GRANDMA'S ATTIC

*W*edding veils date back to Greek and Roman times and are one of the oldest parts of a bridal ensemble. Tradition tells us that the veil was originally worn to prevent evil spirits from thwarting a bride's happiness, or to frighten away spirits. Eventually they were worn to hide the bride's face from the groom, since it was considered bad luck to see the bride before the ceremony.

In Western Christian culture, the veil was eventually used to represent modesty and virginity. It continues, especially in Christian or Jewish cultures, when the bride enters the marriage ceremony with a veiled face and head. She remains fully veiled until the ceremony concludes and either the bride's father or the new groom lifts her veil to reveal her face. The groom often kisses her once the veil is lifted.

For a time, the veil went out of style in Great Britain and North America. However, in 1840, when Queen Victoria married Prince Albert, she wore a veil and it became fashionable once again. Like many things in the Victorian era, the bridal veil became another status symbol. Its weight, length, and quality were an indication of the bride's social status and her family's wealth. The veil was not typically worn over the face until the latter half of the nineteenth century.

Today, the veil is often worn as a simple fashion accessory instead of for its symbolism, though most agree it is an essential piece of the wedding ensemble.

JEFF'S SPAGHETTI PIE

Ingredients:

1 (8 ounce) package
spaghetti noodles,
cooked according to
package directions

1 pound ground beef,
cooked and drained

1 (26 ounce) jar marinara
sauce

2 eggs, beaten

½ cup shredded Parmesan
cheese

8 ounces cottage cheese

2 cups shredded cheddar
and mozzarella cheese

Directions:

Combine ground beef and marinara sauce, set aside.

Place cooked spaghetti noodles in prepared 9 × 13-inch pan.

Pour beaten eggs and Parmesan cheese onto the noodles and
mix.

Layer cottage cheese on top of noodles, followed by marinara
and ground beef mixture. Top with cheese.

Bake for 30 to 35 minutes at 375 degrees.

Let cool 5 to 10 minutes, cut and serve.

Read on for a sneak peek of another exciting book
in the Secrets from Grandma's Attic series!

Turn Back the Dial

By Roseanna M. White

racy Doyle waved to Jana, Matt, Colton, and Natalie with a
wide smile, sending a wink over their heads at Amy and
Miles. She'd been hoping that February would give her—and all of
them, really—time to rest and recuperate after the frantic packing
and moving and wedding prep, but thus far she still felt pretty
exhausted. Even so, she'd volunteered to watch the four kids for the
day while Amy and Miles ran some errands and tackled some
unpacking that hadn't yet been done.

"Thanks again!" her sister called from the sidewalk as she
herded the children toward the car.

Tracy gave one more wave and folded her arms across her
sweater to hold in what warmth was to be found on this chilly
Saturday. "Anytime," she called back. And she meant it. Even if she
did then slip into the house, close the winter out with a shiver, and
breathe a happy, tired sigh.

She didn't regret for a moment helping Amy with the flurry of
packing or planning when she and Matt and Jana had to vacate their

house so quickly. She enjoyed the week the three of them had stayed at her house before the wedding, and had been the first to volunteer to help move their stuff into the Anderson house.

But boy, some of her muscles still ached from the effort, and the thought of hibernating through the rest of winter sounded pretty good right about now.

Of course, if she meant to hibernate, she better have a snack first. She smiled as she breathed in the fragrance of the cookies she'd had Natalie and Jana help her make that morning. The boys had been out in the garage with her husband, Jeff, most of the day, helping him with a shelf he was building, but the girls had both declined. That, she'd decided, was the perfect excuse for breaking out the recipe for the double-chocolate chewy cookies she'd spotted on the internet the week before. Now she breathed in a deep, chocolaty breath and was glad they'd made a double batch. She'd sent most of them home with Amy's crew but still had plenty to enjoy.

She nabbed one now, along with the dregs from the morning's pot of coffee. After popping that into the microwave for a minute, she took cup and cookie into the living room, sank onto the couch with another sigh that made her aware of every one of her years, and bit into the cookie.

Her eyes slid closed as the flavors melted on her tongue. The last few weeks had been nonstop. Ultimately happy but also chaotic. Her heart felt full to the brim as she considered the contentment on her sister's face a few minutes ago when she and Miles had stepped into the kitchen and called for their kids—*theirs*, together. There had already been a few bumps as everyone adjusted to the idea of their new family, and there would be things to sort out yet in terms of details and the realities of six people living together in a house that had previously had only three.

But it would be good. It would be beautiful.

God had created something new.

She must have dozed off for a few minutes after finishing her coffee because she jerked to attention when the door shut, pushing herself up from where she'd somehow ended up cuddled with a throw pillow, Sadie asleep on the floor beside her. Or maybe more than a few minutes. A glance at the clock told her that an hour and a half had slipped by. And the winter sun had gone into hiding while she slumbered the afternoon away.

Whoops. She'd meant to start dinner after she enjoyed her coffee and cookie, not take a nap. Looked like leftovers might be the order of business instead of the chicken and pasta dish she'd been planning.

She stood and followed the sounds of running water to the kitchen, where Jeff was scrubbing his hands at the sink. He tossed a smile at her over his shoulder. "You look like you just had a nice nap."

"Mm?" She lifted a hand to her cheek and felt the dent from the throw pillow there. No doubt her hair was flattened on that side too. Chuckling, she shrugged. "What can I say? It may take me months to recover from January."

Jeff laughed too. "We're not kids anymore, that's for sure. Moving felt a whole lot easier a few years ago. You know what I think we need?"

Leaning a hip against the counter, Tracy made a show of considering. "Pizza? Chinese food? Tacos?"

The tilt of his head said all those options had their merits. "I could be convinced. But I was thinking something bigger. Like a vacation."

"A vacation." She repeated the phrase with a little sigh, this one longing. "That sounds nice." Though with the spring semester underway, that certainly would have to wait. No way would Jeff take a whole week off before spring break. But planning something for then could be entertaining, even refreshing. "Someplace warm, maybe?"

"Maybe." But he didn't say it like he was dreaming of palm trees and white sand beaches. He said it like he had something up his sleeve already.

Tracy straightened again and narrowed her eyes. "What are you planning, Jeffrey Doyle?" Something for their anniversary, perhaps, on Valentine's Day? Though it wasn't like thirty-two years was a typical milestone.

His grin was boyish. "Tell you what. I'll go pick up some dinner for us, and then we can listen to *Turn Back the Dial*, and I'll tell you what I'm thinking."

A frown weighed down Tracy's brows. They'd listened to the twin radio programs broadcast on Saturday nights from Culver-Stockton a few times before—*Jukebox Saturday Night*, which played big band music, and then *Turn Back the Dial*, which aired old radio shows. Dramas, comedies, mysteries. They were entertaining, but they weren't part of their routine by any stretch of the imagination, and they usually listened to them on a whim. They didn't *plan* it.

Clearly Jeff knew something she didn't. "Um…okay."

He toweled his hands dry, still smiling. "I ran into Ken Frost on campus yesterday," he said of the shows' host. "He said they had something fun planned and gave me a little hint of what it was. I promised him we'd tune in. So, takeout?"

Apparently, he wanted her to discover this "something fun" during the broadcast rather than telling her about it now. Well, she could play along with that, especially if it meant getting something for dinner other than the spaghetti in the fridge that she'd already had twice this week. They debated the merits of the various takeout places nearby for a few minutes before deciding on enchiladas. Tracy called in the order at Los Nopales, and Jeff grabbed his keys.

Ordinarily she would have offered to ride along with him, but the kitchen still bore the marks of the cookie baking, so she opted for staying behind and doing some cleanup while he fetched the food.

She went ahead and switched on the aging radio, tuning it to the college's station just in time to hear the music program's adopted theme song, "Jukebox Saturday Night," performed by Glenn Miller and the Modernaires.

While big band music wasn't her daily go-to, she always enjoyed it when it was on. Tonight, it put a swing in her step while she did the dishes, put them and the cookies away, and sidestepped Sadie, who had, of course, plopped herself down in the middle of the floor so she could watch Tracy's every dancing move.

She was filling water glasses when Jeff returned with paper bags in hand. He pulled out chips and salsa and two boxes with enchiladas, Spanish rice, and refried beans that smelled fabulous even before he took the lids off.

"Oh, this was a good idea," she said as she sat, her hand stretched toward Jeff's.

He took her fingers, grinned, and said the blessing.

Tracy had just lifted her first bite to her lips when Ken's convivial voice came on the radio between songs. "And that was tonight's 'Let's Let Bing Sing' selection. Now, as we're bebopping our way to Valentine's Day, I want to remind all of our lovely listeners about our annual Swingin' Gala. This year it'll be held at the old hotel ballroom on the weekend after Valentine's Day, and do we have a treat for you! No, not just live music by Harmony Corner, though that will be a delight. But there will also be a grand announcement of the winner of a contest that I'll give you all the details for in the next hour. So stay tuned through the rest of *Jukebox Saturday Night* and into *Turn Back the Dial*, friends, because you don't want to miss out on this one."

"A contest, huh?" Tracy forked up some rice and sent her husband a probing look. "What kind of contest? Something we'll be good at?"

Jeff laughed around his bite of enchilada, answering only after he'd swallowed. "Oh, honey. This one is right up your alley."

And it had something to do with a vacation, given his initial bringing up of the subject. Interesting, indeed. What sort of contest would have a vacation as a prize?

It was no doubt something small. A weekend at a local B and B or something. She'd never heard of the college's tiny community station doing anything all that grand. It received most of its funding, after all, through grants and donations.

Even so, Jeff's secrecy and grins made her think it would be something fun. Entertaining. And the prize must be desirable if he'd mentioned it like he had.

She probably shouldn't let those visions of palm trees keep swaying in her imagination, but even so. With a salute of her fork, she acknowledged the promise of the contest. "You're not going to tell me anything about it?"

"Ken will tell you soon enough." Jeff scooped some salsa onto a chip, eyes twinkling. "Besides, I don't know the details. Only the gist."

"Fine, fine. Then you'd better distract me. How were Matt and Colton on the latest restoration project?"

Jeff regaled her with tales of the boys' enthusiasm for learning to use a drill and of how carefully Matt had applied the stain to the shelf he was working on. She shared what fun the girls had enjoyed in the kitchen, offering a sample for their dessert. They finished up, put everything away, loaded the dishwasher, and were taking their cookies and glasses of milk into the living room when the hour changed, and the radio program changed with it.

Tracy listened as the intro for *Turn Back the Dial* came on. Honestly, even when they tuned in for the music, she rarely kept it on for the radio show afterward. Listening to the hour's rebroadcast of an old scripted program required too much focused attention, unlike music that could just play in the background while she did something else. Though there had been a couple over the years that she'd enjoyed listening to.

The canned intro faded out, and Ken's voice came over the airwaves again. "Hello, hello, guys and dolls. I hope you're all having a swingin' good Saturday night. Tonight on *Turn Back the Dial*, we're going to be listening to one of the highest-rated shows across the airwaves in 1948—*Windy City Gumshoes*, starring Heath Reynolds and Betty Gardiner as investigative team Joe and Josie, sibling mystery-solvers."

A mystery show. Those tended to have a plot unto themselves that didn't require foreknowledge of the rest of the series. That was nice. A couple of times she'd heard the start of a drama and turned it off simply because she had no idea who anyone was. Tracy dipped her cookie into her milk and then hurried it to her mouth before it could break.

Jeff had already polished off his first cookie, and rather than reach for his second, he instead grabbed a notebook and pen, uncapping the second with a flourish.

Interesting. This would require note-taking. Tracy took a sip of milk and gave Ken's voice her undivided attention.

"*Windy City Gumshoes* came across the airwaves every Friday night at eight from 1946 to 1949, reaching nationwide syndication by the time it went off the air at the end of the decade. And that, guys and gals, is a mystery in and of itself. A mystery *you* are invited to solve."

Jeff had written down the name of the show and of the two starring voice actors, along with the dates.

"In early 1949, the show simply went off the air at the height of its popularity, when its lead voice actor, Heath Reynolds, vanished. What happened to Heath? Why didn't the show continue, bringing in a new actor? Why did all mention of both the actor and the show vanish so quickly from the headlines? These are the questions you're going to answer, and the clues you'll need will be found in the last four episodes of the show itself."

That seemed strange. How could the clues to a real man's disappearance be found in the fictional show he starred in? Tracy pursed her lips as Jeff scribbled that information down.

"Now, I know what you're thinking," Ken continued. "How can the clues be in the show if the mystery is real? Well, my friends, these final episodes, as they turned out to be, were in fact unique. Rather than being recorded in-studio as usual, in a grand publicity stunt, the show hit the road, traveling the very path that the characters took, as they were taking it, week by week. The cast and crew left Chicago and recorded each week's episode in the studio of a local radio station in the town in which the next one was set."

Tracy reached for her phone, pulled up a map, and dropped a pin in Chicago.

"In the show, the sleuths were engaged in a multi-episode mystery, chasing clues from Chicago south to Indianapolis, then cutting west to Peoria and—you guessed it, my friends—right here to Canton, Missouri. Rumor had it that the show and its cast were supposed to end up in Kansas City for the big finale, but they never made it there. The episode recorded here in 1949 was the last one ever to reach the airwaves."

Tracy dropped pins in the locations, tracing the route south and then west. The indirect path would have made for a long day but an easy month, if they only traveled once a week to the next stop.

"All along the way, the stars of the show were met with crowds of enthusiastic fans eager to get a glimpse of the faces that belonged to their favorite voices. And all across America, at-home sleuths tried to put together the same clues as the actors to solve the mystery of the missing coffee heiress…only to end up with the mystery of the missing radio show star."

And if the stars were last seen in Canton, then it could be reasonably surmised that there had been clues to be found here.

Then, anyway. In 1949. But now, seventy-five years later?

"Back in 1949, an investigation was launched, but an answer was never found. An answer there is, though, my friends, and a winner will be drawn from everyone who sends the correct solution to me at Ken at Turn Back the Dial dot com. The winner will win—are you ready for this?—an all-expenses-paid Mississippi River cruise for two to New Orleans! This romantic getaway will be presented to the winning couple at our annual Swingin' Gala at the old hotel ballroom, the Saturday after Valentine's Day. That's only two weeks from now, friends. So get your sleuthing caps out!"

A river cruise? Tracy had always thought one of those would be fun, and she'd been wanting to go to New Orleans for years. She looked over to Jeff and found him smiling at her. Obviously, he knew that. That was why he'd been excited for her to learn about the contest and its prize.

On the radio, Ken launched a bit of celebratory music, giving Tracy the chance to say, "This sounds like fun!" without the fear of missing any details.

"Doesn't it? I bet you can unearth all the old investigation findings in the newspaper's archives, so we'll at least know as much as they did then."

Absolutely. No doubt others in town could learn the same using the library's microfiche collection, but she loved going through the actual archives. And if Ken could promise that the answers existed and he would know the right solution when it came into his inbox, then obviously the clues were there. Someone had found them before now.

"Can't be anything too dire and grisly, right?" Jeff said with a chuckle. "They wouldn't be celebrating a cold-case murder with a river cruise."

"Yeah, that wouldn't scream 'romantic getaway.'"

The music faded out again, Ken's voice taking over. "We'll play one episode a night and cycle through all four, in order, from now until the gala, so if you miss one the first time, you can catch it again four days later. But take care with your answers, friends. You can only turn in *one* solution to these questions: What happened to Heath Reynolds? Why did *Windy City Gumshoes* go off the air? And lastly, why was it forgotten? Are you ready? Here's the show."

More music played, this time with a voice-over that gave the tagline of the show. *In the windy city, mysteries abound, but none whose answer can't be found by this intrepid duo, lovely Josie and her big brother, Joe...*

Music again, and then the sound of footsteps and a squeaking, creaking door. Tracy pulled up a note app on her phone while Jeff drew a line on his paper and wrote *Episode 1* under it. They shared a smile.

Hers grew when Jeff flipped a few pages and showed her what was hidden in the back of his notebook. Two tickets to the Swingin' Gala. He must have purchased them at the college yesterday.

Well. Even if they didn't solve the mystery, they were going to have a fun Valentine weekend. And a mystery to solve would keep the two weeks until then interesting too.

A Note from the Editors

We hope you enjoyed another exciting volume in the Secrets from Grandma's Attic series, published by Guideposts. For over seventy-five years, Guideposts, a nonprofit organization, has been driven by a vision of a world filled with hope. We aspire to be the voice of a trusted friend, a friend who makes you feel more hopeful and connected.

By making a purchase from Guideposts, you join our community in touching millions of lives, inspiring them to believe that all things are possible through faith, hope, and prayer. Your continued support allows us to provide uplifting resources to those in need. Whether through our communities, websites, apps, or publications, we inspire our audiences, bring them together, and comfort, uplift, entertain, and guide them. Visit us at guideposts.org to learn more.

We would love to hear from you. Write us at Guideposts, P.O. Box 5815, Harlan, Iowa 51593 or call us at (800) 932-2145. Did you love *Veiled Intentions*? Leave a review for this product on guideposts.org/shop. Your feedback helps others in our community find relevant products.

Find inspiration, find faith, find Guideposts.

Shop our best sellers and favorites at

guideposts.org/shop

Or scan the QR code to go directly to our Shop